Publicity:
Belinda Harley Associates
1 Blandford Street, W1H 3AA
01 486 9919

PHIL EDMONDS

A Singular Man

PHIL EDMONDS

A Singular Man

SIMON BARNES

THE KINGSWOOD PRESS

Contessa Francesca Elena Maria
di Moriarti-Edmonds

with all my love

P.E.

The Kingswood Press
an imprint of William Heinemann Ltd.
10 Upper Grosvenor Street, London W1X 9PA

LONDON   MELBOURNE   TORONTO
JOHANNESBURG   AUCKLAND

First published 1986

0 434 98092 7

Typeset by Hewer Text Composition Services, Edinburgh
Printed and bound in Great Britain by
Mackays of Chatham Ltd.

CONTENTS

Acknowledgements *vii*
Introduction *ix*
1 African Child *1*
2 English Public Schoolboy *14*
3 Cambridge Cricketer *23*
4 The Ally *36*
5 Snake Balls *49*
6 Chanel No 5 *63*
7 The Good Tourist *81*
8 Hard Times *95*
9 The Dilettante Entrepreneur *107*
10 Team Man *121*
11 Back in the Fold *129*
12 Worldly Wise *139*
13 The Last Great Amateur *145*
Statistical Summary:
Phil Edmonds in First Class Cricket, 1971–85 *169*
Index *177*

Acknowledgements

Phil Edmonds:

My Middlesex C.C.C. and England colleagues.

Cerberus, the gateman at Lord's, for constantly keeping me out of the ground.

Nancy, ace cook at Lord's, much love.

Gray Nicholls and Duncan Fearnley for assisting me in the few runs I have mustered in my career.

Jim Fairbrother, Lord's groundsman, for producing pitches receptive to spin in the mid-seventies.

Cyril Coote, groundsman at Fenners, but much more a father figure for all Cambridge cricketers since the end of the Second World War.

Majid Khan, friend and cricketing ally.

Johnnie Walker and Hine Cognac for easing the pain in India 1984–5 and West Indies 1985–6.

Adrian Murrell, cricket photographer.

Simon Barnes, vegetarian, telephone user and author who has had much with which to put up.

My very loving parents, Douglas James and Marie-Elizabeth Edmonds,

and lastly, Derek Wyatt, my publisher, who finally forced me to sign on the dotted line.

PHIL EDMONDS

Simon Barnes:

Phil Edmonds, for Mexican beers and use of the phone.

Frances Edmonds for spaghetti and slander.

John Pawsey and Derek Wyatt for fixing.

Norman Fox, to whom my debt is unrepayable,

all those who helped the researches, especially David Gower, Mike Brearley, Bob Willis, Paul Downton, and John Kendall-Carpenter. Also Mark Rees for computer-fixing and my wife, Cindy Lee Wright, for assistance that even included laughing at the jokes.

INTRODUCTION

I cannot say that I was overpleased when I was asked by *The Times*, for whom I write as a columnist, to do an interview with Phil Edmonds. Frankly, I felt this was trouble I could do without. It was the beginning of the 1984 season, and it was obvious already that this would be yet another season with Edmonds out of favour. It had never been clear why England selectors had adopted the motto of 'any one, so long as it's not Edmonds', but most people assumed it was because Edmonds was simply too horrible to merit inclusion. It was an interesting subject all right – but it seemed to me to be the sort of story it was more fun to commission than to carry out.

However, we sports journos have to maintain our street cred. You really cannot go to your sports editor and say you would rather not do the story, because you are frightened that Edmonds will be beastly. And it seemed certain that he would be fairly unpleasant: after all, England selectors cannot be wrong so often over 12 or more years, can they?

I couldn't reach Edmonds direct, and so I left a message at Lord's for him to call me. I was happy with that. I felt confident that he would be far too arrogant to pick up the telephone to speak to a mere journalist. 'He didn't call back,' I would tell my boss. 'So sod him, then, eh?'

But Edmonds did call back. It was not reassuring: clipped African vowel-sounds tend to raise the hackles of people who have had a liberal upbringing. Clearly, Edmonds was not only unpleasant, but a rampant white supremacist to boot. I didn't know then that his family had been up to their necks in radical black politics when he was a lad in Zambia, or that one of Edmonds' best dressing-room mates is Wayne Daniel.

So, my bluff having been called, I had to go to Lord's to meet the man. It was April, a couple of weeks before the season started. Edmonds caught my attention from the first: how many slow bowlers appeal every time the ball passes the bat? I mean, in the nets? There he was, bowling with that stately, high-armed action, making remarks like: 'Oh yes, what a beautiful ball!'

When the practice session was over, Edmonds and I went to have lunch in The Tavern. I dug out my note-book and started the interview with care and circumspection: I didn't want to offend this peculiar chap, did I? Not till his back was turned, anyway.

But to my surprise, the interview was not difficult. In fact, it was a cracker. Edmonds was charming, very funny, and recklessly indiscreet. 'Brearley was too namby-pamby for my taste,' he said, while I scribbled furiously and envisaged an award-winning piece.

By the time we had moved onto the second beer, the interview had degenerated into a conversation. He and I began arguing about one thing and another, and later on I found myself sending him up something rotten, and being amiably abused in return. We left The Tavern, to my immense surprise, on a note of splendid, bantering cheerfulness. Here was the greatest monster in English cricket – and I found I actually *liked* the man. Shurely shome mishtake, I thought, as we walked back through Grace Gate.

The piece I later wrote for *The Times* (headlined 'The awkward left hand of England') prompted a few readers to write to say that Edmonds should be back in the England team, another to say he should be banned from cricket for life, and also provoked the Middlesex committee into stern reaction. This was not exactly a novelty for Edmonds. They felt that Brearley would be dreadfully offended by some of his remarks: this too, was not without precedent.

After Edmonds and I had passed through Grace Gate, we took a stroll around the perimeter of the ground, chatting amiably. We came to a halt across the green from the nets, and watched the players at practice: Mike Gatting doing his Heavyweight Skipper bit, Daniel in about 14 sweaters dreaming of sun and Red Stripe.

INTRODUCTION

Edmonds looked at it all for a while and then said casually: 'I've had enough of this.'

'Oh yes?'

'I'll retire at the end of the season. I've had enough.' It was a sad, almost a defeated remark. But 18 months later, he had surfaced to become a fixture in the England team: a vital part of two successive series wins, in India and at home to Australia.

As we watched the practice, with Gatting's voice billowing across to us ('Well bowled Wayn-eeeee!') Edmonds put his hands together and mimed a little iron shot. 'I should have been a golfer,' he said. As a matter of private interest, at that moment I had one of those sudden piercing intuitions, and felt convinced that I would end up writing a book with this strange, and strangely agreeable fellow.

Now I seem to have done so. Most of the sessions we did together took place at his London flat, and the tape recorder took down every detail: the stories, the arguments, the African vowels, the clash of cutlery, the glug of wine bottles, and the slanderous asides from Phil's wife, Frances, who has become almost as famous for indiscreet remarks as her husband. She loves witticisms for their own sake, and would happily, like Oscar Wilde, go to jail for the sake of a good one-liner. 'Cricket has certainly widened my social horizons,' she said. 'I'd never have met a man like **** in normal life – not unless I had a burst pipe, or something.'

Her assessment of the qualities of England cricketers in the pages of the *Daily Express* gave everyone a belly-laugh, but probably got her banned for life from the England Wives Knitting Circle. So far she has managed to take this set-back in her stride.

Edmonds filled the tapes with digressions on the nature of political reality, the way he will make his second million (he is not a man who thinks small), his recollections of friendships and feuds, conflicts and conspiracy, triumphs and disasters and cricket, lovely cricket above all else. 'Play up and play the game – that's the only way to approach cricket,' he said, and if you find it hard to believe, I've got it on tape.

He is a strange man in some respects, but his reputation for beastliness is not based on fact. 'He has the reputation for being awkward and arrogant,' Frances wrote, 'mainly because he is awkward and arrogant.' Well, you can accuse the man of a lot of things, and many people have done. But boring he ain't.

CHAPTER 1

AFRICAN CHILD

Phil Edmonds is a singular man. His cricket career has been extraordinary, characterised by selectorial caprice, unsympathetic handling, and the growth of an unmerited reputation for being a monster of egotism. It is true, however, that Edmonds does not quite fit in with the people around him. He seems to lack a number of the familiar traits and opinions you would expect to find in an Englishman.

The reason for this is simple. Edmonds is not now, nor has ever been, an Englishman. At least, not an Englishman through and through. To carry the Christian names of Philippe Henri tends to make you stand out in a list of English names. To be six foot three and to carry yourself as if you were seven foot four similarly makes you noticeable among the English: a society that tends to encourage a kind of stooping false modesty. No one has ever accused Edmonds of false modesty, however. And even from a distance, you cannot mistake Edmonds for a run-of-the-mill anybody.

He was born in Africa, the son of a Belgian lady (hence the French names) and an Englishman. Phil Edmonds stands out in England: and his entire family stood out in Africa. In fact, they became outcasts from white society. 'Growing up in Africa was magnificent,' Edmonds said. 'The bush, the wide open spaces of the high savannah land, and the beautiful climate gave you an unbelievable sense of freedom. At the same time, the 1950s and 1960s were years of tremendous political change in central Africa. I had the opportunity

1

to see all this from the inside, because of my father's heavy involvement with black politics. But because of that, the Special Branch kept a very close eye on us. It was believed that we were raging communists who received secret coded messages from Moscow hidden in the morning milk.

'My time in Africa has certainly marked me for life. I left when I was 15, but the experiences we had there conditioned many of my attitudes, and determined much of my thinking, my ideas and my political philosophy.'

He was born in Lusaka, which was then the capital of the colony of Northern Rhodesia, and which is now capital of the independent republic of Zambia. The current president of Zambia, Kenneth Kaunda, was a daily visitor to the Edmonds home long before he was a power in the land. Phil remembers taking food to Kaunda's family when he was in jail on Christmas Day. Phil grew up at a time when 'the winds of change', in Harold Macmillan's heady phrase of the time, were sweeping through the continent of Africa. With the benefit of hindsight, it was clear that by the 1950s the days of colonial rule were numbered. But at the time, for most of the white colonials, the notion of black rule was unthinkable, impossible, anathema: the events that brought the end of colonial rule came as a series of frightening shocks to the white population, or most of it. One or two of the whites saw things more clearly. And Phil Edmonds' father did all he could to foster the growth of the emerging black political power.

Philippe Henri was born on March 8, 1951. 'Lusaka was my home town. It was then a one horse town of 20,000 whites. But at the time it was the centre of the universe, and I never wanted to live anywhere else.'

Both the Edmonds parents were convention-flouters. His mother came from a haute bourgeoise family, a family which, Phil complains, still doesn't take him seriously at all. 'To them I am not a bon travailleur, and that is what counts,' he said. 'I am just un joker – un joker qui joue au cricket.' Marie-Elisabeth broke all the traditions of the staid Belgian professional classes when she married a live-wire Englishman after a war-time romance, a man who was something of an intellectual and a great deal of a go-getter: a man enthralled by politics and by business, in that order. Both these preoccupations are shared by his son Phil, but with him the order is

2

reversed. But both men are fascinated by the problems, the nature, and the operation of power.

Phil and his father share a total lack of respect for rank: this is as much a family as a colonial trait. Phil said: 'The old man joined the army, and turned down numerous offers of commissions to become an officer. He seems to have had a similar attitude towards the army and authority generally as did Yossarian in *Catch 22*. When he joined the army, he was given an introductory talk. The officer in charge started pounding the old lectern, telling them what a great unit they were all joining. He went on to tell them how the unit took part in some tremendous battle and how only five of them returned. There was a bit of a pause at this, and then my old man put up his hand. He asked: "Could I please be transferred to another unit? One where 5,000 came back?" It wasn't the kind of mentality to enamour one to the establishment. And I know exactly how he feels of course.

'In the same way, I can't respect a guy just because he has been given some title like "captain". I can respect a guy for what he does, but not for his title. I don't believe I've ever called Mike Gatting (captain at Middlesex) "Skipper". I call him Gatt. Now, Gatt calls David Gower "Skip" at Test matches. I call him "David". I can't go along with the idea that just having the title "captain" makes you a special kind of person. Titles are so important to some people, who seem to imagine that a title of any kind makes a superior being.'

If it was unconventional of Marie-Elisabeth to marry an Englishman, it was even more unusual to go off to Africa (apart from the Congo). Her husband, Douglas Edmonds, went out via Johannesburg to Northern Rhodesia with a construction company. He moved to Lusaka, and liked it: when he was told he would be transferred to the Copperbelt, the mining area in the north of the country on which most of the country's wealth was founded, he refused, resigned and joined another large British construction company. Much of the company's work was building three-roomed houses for the African population: the company was losing £100 with every house they built. Edmonds père turned this into £100 profit. The company, understandably impressed, offered him a contract for life, but Douglas, with an independent streak every bit as strong as his son's, refused – and resigned. He set up in business for himself, with construction interests and a factory producing soft drinks. It was typical of the man that he should decide to take on a monster company like Coca-Cola head-on. However, it was not commercial but political opposition that undid him. Government moves made him a pauper. Later still, he was able to make his fortune all over again: unquestionably, he is an exceptional man.

Phil has powerful memories of the shifting political climate and the fluctuations of the Edmonds fortunes: however, his earliest memories are of running wild. 'We grew up as a large family, but I was particularly close to my brother, Pierre, who was just a year older. He and I used to go out into the bush for hours at a time. Not hunting, not at this stage, we were too young – we were just kids of seven and eight, roaming round the bush, with all the animals. We used to spend hours and hours climbing trees, huge trees 40 and 50 feet tall. The folks would come home and look for us, and find us miles up in the trees – I don't know how we got up so high.

'We had lots of animals, loads of dogs, even a pet pig. We used to roam about everywhere, we swam in all the rivers and were probably riddled with bilharzia. We would pick up stones and chuck them at trees. There were these fruit – we used to call them monkey nuts – that had big seeds inside, and we used to chuck them for hours and hours. By the time we were playing cricket at school, we both had tremendously good arms, all from spending so much time trying to knock the fruit out of the trees.

'We saw the occasional antelope, and the odd duiker, but we didn't see that many wild animals. Kids make too much noise for that. We were among all the local cattle, kept there in a free range situation. It was highland savannah, not forest. There were cows, lots of dogs, thousands of birds, enormous birds of prey and tiny birds like jewels, and millions of snakes: cobras, gaboon vipers, puff adders. It was rather dangerous, when you think of it in retrospect – two kids of seven and eight, out in the bush ten miles from home, catching poisonous snakes and cracking them like whips.'

A true outdoor childhood, one in which every day can be spent roaming in a pair of shorts and a shirt, is something that the average Brit, used to this miserable climate, has no conception of. It was almost impossible not to be vigorous and hearty and sporty: there was so much opportunity to be outdoors playing sports, and so little opportunity for anything else. It was something the Edmonds brothers took as a natural part of life: when they went to their high school later on, they would cycle there and back, a distance of 10 miles each way. They would also cycle home for lunch and cycle back to play sport every afternoon. The idea of taking sandwiches never occurred to them. 'I can remember regularly walking five miles to buy a copy of the *Central African Post*,' Edmonds said. 'Can you imagine walking five miles to get the London *Evening Standard?* And this paper wasn't even as good as the *Evening Standard.*' It is hardly surprising that the Edmonds brothers grew up to be enormous, strapping lads with legs like tree trunks, and when it came to throwing the cricket ball, their only rivals in the school were each other.

In their junior school days, when Pierre and Phil were not wandering about the bush, they were playing cricket. They had an enormous garden: space is easy to get hold of in a big developing country. Neighbours, however, are not so readily available, so the Edmonds brothers had only each other as opponents. Naturally this was no bar to staging England v South Africa Test matches in the back garden. 'We were used to listening to the cricket commentaries on the BBC World Service. So when we played, we also did the ball by ball commentaries: Pierre was Charles Fortune, and I was Rex Alston. And we'd also be the entire England or the entire South Africa Test team. All the trees would be fielders, we would set up wheel barrows and buckets to take catches. Any time we weren't in the bush, we'd be playing cricket in the garden, just the two of us, all day long, playing cricket and doing the commentary.'

The Edmonds were part of a white society in a black country: but there was no question or even any chance of living in isolation from the black population. 'The old man had a brick-making business at one stage, and Pierre and I used to spend a lot of times with the Africans, making bricks with them. But we were always conscious of the black-white divide – it was something you were aware of very early. You knew that simply by being white, you were privileged. It wasn't that you didn't have anything to do with the Africans. A lot of kids had black nannies, and would spend more time with the black family than with their own – but there was still always the divide. Even when you were very young, you knew that.'

Later, Phil went to Gilbert Rennie High School, the only high

5

school in Lusaka. 'It was an absolutely magnificent school where the facilities, academic and sporting, were extraordinary – and all for £3 a year. I suppose, looking back, that it set itself up to create the leaders of tomorrow: the basic Oxbridge philosophy of education. Indeed, most of the masters were Oxbridge, and the main cricket field was called Parker's Piece after the cricket field in Cambridge. Academic streaming was ruthless, and discipline, by English standards, was incredibly harsh. Can you imagine being beaten for taking a leaf off a tree – because "if everybody did the same the tree would be denuded"? When I went to school in England later on, I could not believe the insolence, and the general disregard that many students seemed to have for their teachers – or that the teachers stood for it. But Gilbert Rennie wanted to make you both a gentleman and a man's man. When boys had disputes, they were settled by boxing matches in the quad. I had my share of these: put on the gloves, fight it out, and forget it.'

Even while Phil was growing up, a long time before he went to the high school, the country was changing. The balance of power between the white colonists and the black natives was beginning to alter. Most of the white population closed their mind to this possibility, to the ghastly, impossible notion of black rule and independence. But Douglas Edmonds was not only fascinated by the early indications – the early hopes – of change. He also did everything he could to encourage the changes. And for his family, the awareness of powerful political forces became part of the daily rhythms of life.

Most of the Edmonds' white neighbours were violently opposed to any impending changes – to the extent they were aware of them – but not for patriotic, British-type reasons. A new kind of patriotism grows up in the overseas Britisher: even today, you can find this strong colonial attitude, in such places as Hong Kong, where I lived for some years. Many long-term Hong Kongers do not call England 'home': they say 'UK'. Hong Kong is home. This was unquestionably the attitude of the colonials of Africa: they were not the here-today-gone-tomorrow sort. And like the Hong Kongers, they developed a new attitude to the people in the 'UK'. They saw such people – the stay-at-homes – as just a little soft, as somehow lacking in vigour, self-reliance, go-getting spirit: all the traditional colonial virtues. Thus overseas Brits often feel more committed to their adopted country than to the 'UK'. Often they will have been born and educated thousands of miles from London. In times of trouble – as Hong Kongers faced over the 1997 question – they grow horrified at the notion that all can be lost at the caprice of some politician back in England: someone who does not know the country and who therefore cannot possibly 'understand'. A wariness of all leaders from the 'UK' is inevitable. Then follows a growing suspicion that colonials are expendable, and available for sale down the river if their country grows troublesome to London. British colonials will tend to be just a little anti-British. And because they are the men on the spot, the colonials 'know' that change is impossible – unthinkable.

But Douglas Edmonds was a man who did, in fact, think the unthinkable. Indeed, he encouraged it. He became aware of the growing determination of well-educated blacks to become involved in the running of their country. The notion may have been anathema to the old Africa hands, but Edmonds père believed that black rule was natural, inevitable, and right. Accordingly, the Edmonds house became the place where ambitious, politically aware blacks could meet, and discuss ideas and plans with the remarkable, prescient white man, Douglas Edmonds. 'I remember when I was very young, back in the 50s, we often had social functions at home that were completely multi-racial. This was extremely unusual for the time. Kenneth Kaunda; Simon Kapwepwe; James Skinner, who became attorney-general; and men like these – were all daily guests in my father's house.

'I think my father had a great deal that was sympathetic to them. Firstly there was his liberalism – his belief that all men were equal, and that naturally everyone should have a say in governing his country. Secondly, there was the mistrust of the British, which my father, and many other white Northern Rhodesians, shared. The period of 1950–65 was an interesting one. Northern Rhodesia, Southern Rhodesia and Nyasaland were joined together in 1951 to form the Federation of Rhodesia and Nyasaland. This was really a device to transfer the wealth of the Copperbelt in Northern Rhodesia down to the more established south. This became so transparent that Salisbury, the capital of Southern Rhodesia, was known as Bamba-Zonki – which means "grab everything". Then we had a gradual development of black political awareness that

7

culminated in the breakaway of Hasting Banda's Malawi in 1963 and the independence of Zambia on October 1964. Throughout all this, it was fascinating to watch the political manoeuvrings of the British establishment, which was far too sophisticated and hypocritical for the local yokels – black and white. It was also interesting to watch the development of the church as it moved from a seemingly reactionary body to an extremely radical one.

'Our family was able to watch much of this from the inside. My father was an idealist, a man who believed in good "Christian" virtues – that all men should be given equal opportunity, and that one should behave "properly" in life and do what was "right": surely we must try to develop a system to give all men equal opportunity; surely it is wrong to pinch all the wealth from the north for politically expedient reasons. Inevitably, these unfashionable views caused the white governing establishment – including the church – much distress. And inevitably, this cemented a relationship with the so-called radical thinkers and threw us deeply into black politics. The economic and social consequences of this were detrimental in the extreme. However, a large family of five children (three boys and two girls), with loving parents, is a pretty resilient entity. It needed to be.'

The official response to Douglas Edmonds' growing involvement with the emergent black politicians was devastating. It ruined him. His soft-drinks factory was forced into liquidation. He still had interests in construction, but he was unable to secure work or contracts of any kind. Most of his business interests went to the wall. They were left with his mother's small salary as a teacher in Gilbert Rennie High School – that, and a small amount of sympathy and support. As a bonus, the Edmonds family – from father down to youngest son – were treated almost as social lepers by most of the white community.

'The family became known as "the kaffirboeties" – the black-lovers. We were socially unacceptable. When we went to school, inevitably, there were plenty of fights. Pierre and I often needed the protection of our elder brother, Jean-Daniel. As far as we were concerned, it was the Edmonds brothers back-to-back against the world. At home we were isolated: the family led a virtually self-contained existence for a good four or five years. By the time we went to High School in the early 1960s, things had just begun to change, the hostility to us was beginning to wane. By then the writing was on the wall.'

One of the people who helped the family to keep going in the period when there was scarcely any money coming into the house, was the local grocer, a Greek. He used to supply the Edmonds' with 10 pints of milk and five French loaves every day. 'The man who lived next door to us was a good, solid Afrikaaner Special Branch man. He saw all the bread and milk coming in every day, and so reported that we were getting coded messages from our communist bosses in Russia, hidden in the loaves and bottles. We were thought to be in the pay of the communists: and this stuff about secret messages was sent back to London. The old man was thought to be a dangerous guy – all for believing in good "Christian virtues".

'But throughout it all, we – the kids – just took it all for granted. All the black politician guys, they were just buddies of my father's. It never occurred to us that the old man should act differently. It was an interesting time for us, in fact. Even at that time, I found the relationship between Kaunda and Kapwepwe fascinating. Kapwepwe always seemed to be more radical, saying: "Look, we must do more for the people".' It was, of course, Kaunda who became the first, and so far the only president of the new nation, Zambia, which finally achieved independence in October '65, when Edmonds was 14. Kapwepwe was later put in detention by Kaunda.

While you probably won't find the name of Douglas Edmonds in any official history books, he was undoubtedly a catalyst for black rule in an independent Zambia. It is a role that any one might be proud of: if Douglas Edmonds feels pride, it is the only prize he won for his long-term dedicated support of Kaunda and Co. He was the man who helped Kaunda more than any one else. Yet when it came to dishing out the rewards, when Kaunda was finally in charge, he got nothing. He was not the sort to expect much, of course, nor was he thinking of rewards at any time during his involvement with Kaunda. But he was disappointed to be taken completely for granted after independence. 'My old man went to Kaunda once and asked him what was going on. "Look, these guys were ready to shoot you a few months ago. Now you're keeping them in power, giving them plum jobs and plum contracts, for road-building and what have you. What about me?" And the response was: "Well, we take you for granted. You're one of us. But these others – we need to keep them happy!"'

If Douglas Edmonds was an idealist, Kaunda was a realist: a practical politician, a man interested in making things work, not in pursuing abstract goals. Phil Edmonds, a young and fascinated onlooker, saw, and learned. 'Expediency is what rules', he says now, 'not nice liberal ideas. That is the traditional hypocrisy of the world. Not of Black Africa, but of the world: it happens every-where, and all establishments are the same. If the Soviets took over England tomorrow, the infrastructure of the country would remain exactly the same. The people who run the trains and the roads would carry on, and so, of course, would the police, the information officers and the MI5 boys. They would hold on to their positions and would be rewarded for doing so. They would do the same job for different masters without a qualm: they'd stay in their positions of power and influence. Exactly the same way that it happened in Africa.'

To grow up at the hub of the turning wheel throughout these years of enormous political change made for an extraordinary childhood. Phil Edmonds could not grow up into anything but a singular man after such an upbringing. He saw a close friend of the family rise from jailed outcast to national leader. He saw his father's position change from trusted friend and adviser to something like an embarrassment. The result was that Edmonds became what he would term a political realist. Those brought up in less strenuous political circumstances would prefer the term cynic. Edmonds, however, does not think that it is cynical to come to terms with the way the world works. The conspiracy theory of history is one that strikes a resounding sympathetic chord in Edmonds' nature: and every angle from which he examines this theory is confirmed by his own childhood experiences of politics.

Cynical does not mean bitter. He doesn't bear resentment on his father's behalf against the politicians of Africa. He does not consider that he or his family have been the victims of malice, or even of circumstance. They have rather been the victims of their own political naïveté, or, at least, by his father's decision to prefer ideals to realpolitik. This was not naïveté in the strict sense: his father showed quite exceptional political prescience and saw that black rule was not only right but inevitable when most white colonials saw it as an impossible nightmare. And this prescience, these memories of being at the very heart of momentous changes, gave Phil Edmonds a sense of privilege: 'Even at the time when we were young, in our early teens, we were interested in the ramifications of all the political changes we had been so closely involved with. And I certainly felt a great sense of the privilege of having had the insight, through my father, that things must change.'

If Africa made Phil Edmonds a political realist, it also made him a religious cynic, and here he would not quarrel with the word. By extension, he is cynical – or at least, extremely realistic – about the church's role in the world, and particularly in Africa. 'My mother is Catholic, but I lapsed at a very early age. I actively resented the fact that we had to go to church on Sunday mornings. When we got there he was to witness the total hypocrisy that went on: the women at the front looking good and the fathers at the back, sitting on the steps reading the Sunday papers. I think it would be fair to say that I lapsed from the moment I first saw what was going on. Every Sunday was a battle to get us to church on time. Pierre and I would be wanting to go out into the bush, shooting or fishing or whatever, and my mother would be going round the house shouting and looking for us. It was always a big hassle and my mother would arrive at church feeling really cross. An hour later, of course, she would emerge relaxed and radiant – I suppose that is what worship is about: an opportunity for quiet and meditation.

'But I could never take it seriously. We had a priest called Father Murphy, who played golf and got tired and emotional too often. He had an operation for gall-stones. I couldn't take him seriously. And I look on the church's involvement in Africa in the same way that I look at political movements. The church operates with the same kind of expediency that every establishment does. Once the writing was on the wall, the church reacted very quickly to establish a future power base – even to the extent that when there was about to be a police raid on black activists, it was rumoured that the church would supply air tickets to the men who they thought were the future civil servants. Lately I've been reading that the church is cautiously saying that there is validity in some animistic practices – you know, worship of the sun and the wind. A few years ago that was seen as paganism pure and simple. But like every establishment, the church has got to evolve if it is to retain its power. In the same

11

way the church used to look on black political movements with horror. Now you can find churchmen giving their support to guerilla movements. Of course they are, it is inevitable that they are – so how can you not be aware of the realities?

'Because of my time in Africa, I am a realist, or a cynic if you prefer. My father has remained idealistic. He would be more cynical, perhaps – but he cannot change his outlook. But it is because of my father's idealism that I am a realist. I cannot watch any television programme with any kind of political implications without wondering about the motive behind it. Indeed, my father will share *that* cynicism: like me, he will wonder what the guy is really trying to gain. He is as cynical as I am in that way. And yet, if he started all over again in Africa, he would undoubtedly do the same thing all over again.'

Though the ending of colonial rule did not bring vast rewards and plum contracts sweeping down on the Edmonds household, Douglas Edmonds was at least able to work again. Being an energetic and imaginative business, he was rapidly able to make his family secure again. The subsidies from the Greek grocer were no longer required: the family prospered. Phil and Pierre were by this time at Gilbert Rennie High School, and both were doing well. Both were games players of immense talent, and both were successful academically, particularly Phil. But as Zambia developed as an independent country, much of the white population was on the move. One reason for this was education. In the first year after independence 25 black boys – the sons of the elite, naturally – joined Gilbert Rennie. The following year, there were to be another 400. One of the first intake once said to Phil: 'Have to leave this school, man – too many damn blacks.' Many whites moved down into Southern Rhodesia and the Ian Smith UDI government. Others moved further south, into what is now Africa's last enclave of white supremacy: South Africa. But the Edmonds family, which lacked generations-old ties to the continent of Africa, made the decision to return to England. The white man's days in Africa were almost over. 'But the idea of going back to England was horrendous. We talked about it for a long time, and in the end it was forced on us. Pierre and I – we didn't want to go at all.'

The mark of Africa, and of that strange political childhood, remains with him. The anglicisation of Phil Edmonds has never been complete. He still speaks with some of the vowels of the white men of Southern Africa. But he lacks the narrowness of vision of the traditional old Africa hand as much as he lacks the traditional narrowness of the English public schoolboy he became. His appreciation of realpolitik; his experience of political isolation in Zambia; his sense of having been granted a privileged insight into the heart of practical affairs; could not but remain with him.

He brought other items with him in his mental baggage when he moved to England. He retains the traditional colonial impatience with the weediness of English responses: he instantly loathed the limp plumping for second best that is so much a feature of British life. He despised the narrow ambitions, the near horizons, the parochialism, the lack of vigour. Above all, he dislikes the pretence that public affairs are performed for vaguely noble motives, the belief that the establishment does not exist for self-serving ends.

Edmonds does not feel shackled by English modesty, or by English reluctance to put himself forward. His temperament is open, aggressive, optimistic, and determined and this determination to make what he chooses from himself is something that comes forward in both his cricket and his business life. In both spheres of action he has had his successes.

To see Edmonds on song, bowling well in a Test match, is to see a man revelling in his gifts and in what he has made of them. But his career has been marked by terrible reverses. Being a realist, or a cynic, he has never been surprised by this. And along with his sense of political realism, he also brought back from Africa a subtle sense of superiority, and a boundless self-reliance. The qualities brought him up from the cricketing pits to which he had been condemned, back to become a topline strike bowler for England. But his boundless cynicism about the motives of men has not changed: nor has he had any experiences to convince him that it should.

CHAPTER 2

ENGLISH PUBLIC SCHOOLBOY

Phil Edmonds should have been made captain of England a long time ago. I obtained this information from Phil himself, who at the same time told me that he was 'the nicest guy in the world'. You can't argue with facts like these.

Bizarre as this may seem, Edmonds' candid self-assessments are not universally accepted. He is an unusual man who possesses many talents, but the gift of easy friendship is not one of them. He does, however, have a remarkable gift for emnity. Not that it is he who collects enemies. It is always other people who tend to collect him as an enemy. Just as Buster Keaton was able to walk wide-eyed and innocent through a landscape, unaware of the chaos as buildings collapsed all around him, so Edmonds carries cheerily on his way, unaware that the road behind him is littered with sensitive souls who have taken mortal offence at some action or word he has let fall. While the offended multitudes see a vicious knowingness, Edmonds retains a kind of innocent bewilderment that people could act so strangely. Edmonds can so often be chilling, prickly, aloof, that people take it personally. People by the score think he has selected them, and them alone, for contempt. But Edmonds is far more democratic than that.

He unquestionably has a gift for alienating people, but being loved has never been a requirement of the job of England captain.

Indeed, to court love and affection is a classic route to disaster for men promoted from the ranks – as England captains almost always are. By no means everybody loved Mike Brearley: nor Douglas Jardine, for that matter: and Edmonds would always incline more towards autocracy than mateyness.

Indeed, Edmonds looked like England captaincy material for years. His talent was never in question: the transitions were all made with ridiculous ease: from schoolboy to university cricketer, from university to county pro, from Middlesex to Test matches. It was all laughably easy. So was his progress in authority: school captain, Cambridge captain, Middlesex vice-captain . . . the road looked clear. It was just a question of time.

There are a million reasons why this didn't happen, and two of them were Derek Underwood and, surprise, surprise . . . Philippe Edmonds. Underwood was considered for years the better left-armer. And when he went AWOL, first with Packer and then with the South African Breweries XI, a new philosophy was born in the hearts of the selectors: 'Keep Edmonds out'. More of that anon; let us for the moment take it that the Edmonds nature caused the selectors to view him with terrible suspicion. Dislike of Edmonds as a pheno-menon was used to mask his talents, keep him from the England side, and from any dreams he might once have held of captaining England. 'Very fine player, of course . . .' they said, their voices fading away, leaving a welter of things unsaid. Nothing concrete, just a vague feeling that there was something *wrong* about Edmonds.

Edmonds' great gift is for conflict. Perhaps he has had the gift throughout his life. Certainly he had it by the time he was at school in England. His relationship with trouble is no casual flirtation: it is a life-long romance. That is why his captaincy of his school cricket team was regarded as a disaster, and it was becausse of his captaincy that his headmaster, John Kendall-Carpenter, was forced to make one of the most unpleasant decisions of his life.

The Edmonds at last left Zambia in 1966. Phil watched the World Cup while staying with his mother's relatives in Belgium, and wondered why they were all cheering for West Germany. The family went on to England, and set up base in Kent. Phil and Pierre were sent to Skinner's School in Tunbridge Wells, which should have been a sticky and traumatic time for this pair of African-bred boys. Kent is not dreadfully African, after all. Phil found the

15

transition reasonably easy. But Pierre had an unspeakable time, and suffered the incessant mockery of a particularly horrible school teacher – 'the sort of small-minded, mean-spirited person that is the kind of Englishman I despise,' Edmonds said – who did not care for a wild colonial boy like Pierre. Pierre soon left for a minor public school, also in Kent, called Cranbrook, where he was at once a roaring success.

Phil remained at Skinner's to do his O levels, and he collected a sickening number thereof ('Dunno how many, 12 or so I suppose . . .') which was fair enough. Sport was, however, less simple. 'They were terrible, they were horrible, they couldn't catch the ball . . . it was very, very frustrating.' But relief was in sight: a team of Zambian schoolboys came to England on a tour, under the name of the Zambian Eagles. Naturally Edmonds knew them all, naturally they asked him to join them. They were mostly 18 year olds, and good players, but Edmonds, though a mere 16, was not about to be overawed. He had a splendid time: 'We travelled round the country whipping all these guys,' he said. They left a trail of hammered public school sides behind them. Perhaps this was not the best possible preparation for English public school life. By the time he joined his brother at Cranbrook, his colonial impatience with the stay-at-home English, and his own self-confidence, were quite gloriously reaffirmed.

Cranbrook was not quite prepared for Phil Edmonds. 'We thought we were getting another Pierre,' said Kendall-Carpenter. 'Pierre was a great blast of warm, friendly air, a big fellow with a chopped-off grin, very amiable, a trifle woolly, and an absolutely splendid chap. I expected another Pierre, but Phil was tempered steel.'

If the headmaster was impressed, his schoolfellows were simply awed. Adolescence is a troubled time for most of us, but Phil looked as if he had reached puberty in one effortless bound. He was enormously tall, and broad to match. Children brought up abroad tend to have a precocious air of grown-upness about them, a confidence at dealing with the real world, something which the home-grown child acquires only with utmost pain and difficulty. The gulf between 16 and 18 seems immense, cataclysmic, to a schoolboy. But at 17 you might well have taken Phil for 25. Even now, in his middle thirties, he has the quite unconscious knack of making people his own age feel like children. At school, he seemed already an adult, with a man's body, a man's worldliness, and a man's abilities. As if that wasn't enough, he had chillingly good looks as well: 'A blond Adonis,' said his cricket master, James Bradnock.

Pierre was a much-loved extrovert, a 'character', a kind of school mascot, especially when he captained the school rugby side as a bull-shoving number eight.

Edmonds minor, however, was not about to get a reputation for amiable woolliness. While Pierre acquired a nickname, Amos (for reasons no one can remember, suggesting only that he had the immensity and ruggedness one might associate with an Old Testament prophet), there was no question of giving Phil a nickname. He was far too grand. 'I remember the stiff back, clear eye, the good-looking, intelligent face,' said Kendall-Carpenter. 'He was very direct, but very courteous. Never anything but courteous. And with women on the staff, he was nothing less than courtly, with old-fashioned manners, very much the gentleman.' Indeed, today Edmonds tends to treat women in an immensely elaborate fashion, if not exactly with courtliness. He blends a ludicrous amount of charm with relentless teasing. He seems to regard women as an altogether separate, though in the main admirable species: certainly one which demands completely different rules of behaviour.

Not only was Edmonds tall, worldly and an exceptional games player: he had intelligence too. He might well have got a scholarship to Cambridge, had being good at all sports not eaten into studying time. It is small wonder that the myth of the Edmonds arrogance began: on a natural bedrock of colonial self-assertiveness he had his stature, and his physical and mental abilities. 'Do you know the one thing I can't stand about this country?' he once said to Bradnock. 'The way it is always glad to accept the second-rate.' This at 17.

Naturally, he was whizzed straight into the school rugby XV, playing at full back or centre while Pierre roared his forwards on. 'Pierre could have gone on to play number eight for England,' said Kendall-Carpenter, who, as former president of the Rugby Football Union, knows what he is talking about. Phil took over as number eight when Pierre left to go to university in South Africa, where he continued to play good rugby but gave the game up when he started working.

Phil also played good quality rugby, and rather revelled in the way a number eight can control a game. They won all their matches in that season, and you can't really ask for more than that. But Edmonds later remarked to Bradnock that he didn't really enjoy rugby. 'You wouldn't have thought that from watching him play the game,' said Bradnock. 'Unless, of course, you had seen him play cricket first.' The school had the makings of a pretty useful cricket side, and Edmonds was put in charge of it. It was an experience he found deeply frustrating. 'The guys just didn't have a clue,' he said.

But then Edmonds was head and shoulders above his colleagues, literally as well as in every cricketing sense. Naturally he was the best bowler, already a prodigious spinner of the ball, and unplayable at that level. He was also capable of bowling a quicker ball that, off five paces, was as fast as anything opposing batsmen had ever seen, even if it wasn't always strictly accurate. He was also the best batsman in the side, which will give current observers a bit of a giggle. He was, in short, a marvellous asset to the school: 'He was everything you could want in a pupil: highly intelligent, highly organised, and an immensely skilled games player,' his headmaster said.

But Edmonds was naturally aloof, self-cast as outsider even as a schoolboy. 'Neither Pierre nor I were great participators,' Edmonds said. 'I think that may have been to do with our Zambian upbringing. We were natural outsiders. I didn't go out and join clubs, I just wouldn't find it natural to participate. In the same way, I wouldn't think of joining the Rotary Club, or the Lions, or even of being a regular at the local pub. Some people are natural joiners, but I'm not one of them. We'd got used to being outsiders in Zambia, as the kaffirboeties, the black-lovers, and we stayed that way in England.

'It was absolutely crazy in retrospect. I mean, the facilities at school were amazing. You could do anything from music to flying – why didn't I join the air force section of the Combined Cadet Force and learn to fly? I could have done that, absolutely free. It was crazy. But I just didn't join. Similarly, I didn't join in, when they guys on the rugby coach at Cambridge would sing dirty songs on the way home. It wouldn't have seemed natural to do so.'

But somehow the playing of team games seemed wholly natural – indeed, to captain the cricket side seemed simply to be a process of natural selection. But then came the day when Kendall-Carpenter was forced to make this difficult and unpleasant decision. He decided to replace Edmonds as captain of the school cricket team.

The root of the problem was that Edmonds was too good – and unable to come to terms with the fact that every one else around him was bad. As captain, he found the shortcomings of his colleagues real torture. It was his precocity that was the problem. At 17, he was virtually capable of playing county cricket – he was to go on and play a few games for Kent seconds that summer. To play schoolboy cricket was agony, almost unbearable. He could not stomach the fact that schoolboy standards were so far below his own. In Zambia, he had played for his school, Gilbert Rennie, and they competed in a men's league. There were no other schools to play against – and the boys were certainly good enough to give the very useful Zambian club cricketers a decent game. The drop in standards from a tremendous men's league to matches against minor public schools was enormous, and in its way, traumatic. Edmonds was no longer playing with equals – he was the best cricketer by miles. This did not make him swanky, it made him furious. He took his own excellence for granted.

Kendall-Carpenter recalled: 'He was an honest bloke. And his honesty included a complete inability to hide his feelings. If a player half-missed a ball, Phil would react, show disgust, and the next time that player went to field a ball, it would go straight through his legs. It was not that Phil was demonstrative, or would shout. His response would be small, but obvious. He would raise an eyebrow, or lift his hands a few inches in a half-arrested gesture of despair. And that would make the poor boy even less effective than before.' Edmonds, gigantic, grown-up and immensely skilled, must have been an awesome sight to a dogged schoolboy duffer who knew he had let the skipper down. 'I'm sure he scared the daylight out of the little boys in his house quite inadvertently. Phil was unable to come to terms with the amateur approach of his colleagues. His standards were absolute; he had defined targets and clear objectives. But he gave me what was really was one of the worst decisions I have had to make.'

'It was immaturity on my part,' Edmonds said. 'I got so frustrated with everybody . . . they couldn't catch the ball, and I'd go berserk. They found it difficult to tolerate me as captain, since I was always bollocking them, and giving them the impression that I thought they were useless . . . and they were useless, as I remember.'

Edmonds lacked the charity and/or imagination to see that his team-mates were doing their best, and that while they were not as good as he was, he was stuck with them. 'His brother Pierre used to josh him the whole time, there was always a lot of banter between them,' Bradnock said. 'I think Phil missed that when Pierre had gone. There was no one left who would dare to josh Phil. If Phil dropped a catch at practice, Pierre would lay into him. There was no one to do that by the time Phil was captain. He was so big, so mature, far more man than boy.'

Kendell-Carpenter, being that sort of headmaster, would not think of delegating the job of giving Edmonds the sack. He found it an immensely disconcerting experience. 'He seemed to be interviewing me. He had accepted the fact and rationalised it while I was still floundering around in a surfeit of words. I expect he wrote me off at once as an old bumbler.' Edmonds said: 'At first I thought: OK, fair enough. Then I thought, this is crazy! How can I not be captain when the other guys are a load of no-hopers?'

Kendall-Carpenter added: 'The problem was in other people's susceptibilities.' That was, and still is, at the heart of the Edmonds 'problem'.

Hah! Obviously Edmonds is unsuited for any form of captaincy at any level and always has been! That is the instant conclusion to jump to here. It is, however, a little bit too easy an option. The difficulty shown by the little episode of the lost captaincy is the problem of coming to terms with the body and the talent of a 25 year old when you have the spiritual resources of a 17 year old. If any one can find an England cricket captain who sailed through adolescence without making a spectacular balls-up somewhere along the line, I will be amazed and recommend deeper research. The problem was that Edmonds simply had not grown into his talent. His spikey nature made it a serious problem, at least for his colleagues.

The school captaincy episode, though interesting, does not say the final word on Edmonds' fitness for captaincy. Not only did he go on to captain Cambridge, but he has been approached informally by a number of counties in recent years, with captaincy playing a part in the discussions. These counties include Worcestershire, Hampshire and Leicestershire. It must be stressed that these were not poachings, or even discussions based on serious figures and dates, but explorations of possibilities, and for one reason or another, Edmonds rejected these chances of captaincy and opted to stay at Middlesex every time, and, being Edmonds, will occasionally relish all his regrets at such missed opportunities. But Edmonds as captain remains and, barring the quite extraordinary, will remain a treat the county championship has missed.

'I think he would make a good leader of professionals,' said Kendall-Carpenter. 'His tactical brain is as good as anybody's. It was not that he lacked leadership. It was just that his leadership came from competitive competence, and we were small stuff.'

Edmonds may have been too grown-up for school cricket, but he enjoyed playing club cricket for a superior village side from Ashford in Kent. 'For a start, I didn't have any expectations of the old buffers who are the weak links in any village team,' Edmonds said. Both he and Pierre played in the side, and did well. The captain there was a farmer called George Brown who won Phil's admiration by pulling a perfect con trick on him. 'It came to harvest time and shunting straw bales onto stacks, and he had about a million of them. One day at the cricket, he said to me and my brother: "I bet you can't lift those bales". We said: "Course we can! No problem!" We ended up lifting a million bales onto his trucks. Then he gave us five pounds – he conned us totally. Nice old boy.'

After the summer of the captaincy affair, Edmonds stayed on an extra term to sort out his Cambridge entrance, after which the school saw him go. Kendall-Carpenter said: 'I feel a great deal of affection for Pierre . . . and a great deal of admiration for Phil. I remember how disconcerting it was, when I told him that he was to be relieved of the captaincy. He is always assessing you, flicking an eye over you, always look down on you from some well-chosen vantage point. He is always the one who chooses the ground.'

Sometimes it seems that Edmonds conversational technique is based on a horrible, calculating seeking-out of your own weaknesses – but Edmonds withdraws himself from people because he's Edmonds, not because you're you. People complain that Edmonds acts superior: the trouble is that he has an unconscious knack of making people feel inferior. In fact, he tends to like people who do not buy his act: Frances, his wife, mocks him unmercifully. It has never occurred to Ian Botham that Edmonds, or anybody, is acting high and mighty. Botham doesn't notice that sort of thing and gets on well with Edmonds in a noisy, bantering way. And the England captain Edmonds always got on best with was Geoffrey Boycott, whose unsubtle joshing in the nets and on the pitch brought the best out of Edmonds. Boycott is always seen as one of the worst captains England ever had – even in an emergency – but he was able to establish something that the captaincy guru, Mike Brearley, was never able to achieve: a splendid, positive relationship with Edmonds. But then Edmonds and Boycott are both undeniably singular men.

When school was over, Edmonds found himself with that priceless gift that comes to all who stay a seventh term in the sixth form: a year off between school and university. This can be a glorious, formative, exploratory period. He played no cricket at all in that summer, but instead, hitch-hiked around Europe and had the usual adventures. And there were other excitements in store for the blond Adonis. Ahead of him lay Cambridge: not just a palace of delights, but one where they play first class cricket in the summer term as well. The enfant looked more doré than ever as he hitched by easy stages back to England.

CHAPTER 3

CAMBRIDGE CRICKETER

There are some sportsmen who see life as an endless series of peaks: one after another must be conquered. Each advance in their sporting career is a kind of victory over the doubts of the multitude, a victory for the sportsman's strident inner determination to show 'em all that he really *is* the best. When such a sportsman looks back, he sees a series of precipitous cliff-faces – every one of which he has climbed with his teeth.

This is not true of Phil Edmonds. At birth, it seems, he stepped onto the up escalator. His ascent from schoolboy to international cricketer was not so much painless as serene. It never occurred to him that he was *not* the best, it never crossed his mind that he should employ anything as sordid as true grit to convince others of his worth. He knew that his worth was shiningly apparent for all to see. He has always seen himself as a natural member of the elite. He was born a white Zambian: obviously, part of that country's elite. He was a member of a family that saw the country's political changes long before the rest: the sense of being a person with a privileged insight into the way of things has stayed with him ever since. At school, he was taller, cleverer and better at games than any one else.

He had no trouble in winning an ordinary place at Cambridge, and so, unsurprised, moved on to pursue his education among the elite of his adopted country. He had planned to read medicine, but he changed direction. Instead, he read land economy. This dismayed some people: land economy is sometimes seen as a kind of thicko-sportsman's degree like geography – a course for which you are ineligible unless you have football studs growing out of the soles of your feet. But Edmonds was not going for the easy option: by this time he had found his fascination with land, with property, and with the world of business. He was, in this area at least, very much his father's son. It was in land, property and business that he saw his long-term future. But in the meantime, he saw no reason not to play a bit of cricket. Surprisingly, he fell into cricket almost by accident and has stayed on for 15 years, even though the property business could so easily have become an all-absorbing occupation.

'I have never thought of life in terms of a series of goals,' Edmonds said. 'I have never thought of boundaries I must reach – I must do this by the time I'm 25, or what have you. I have just travelled on from one thing to the next: O levels, A levels, university, cricket . . . I have never sought to achieve any particular goal, just to fulfill myself in what I am doing at the time.'

Frances said: 'In a way, it would have been better if you had been like young Nigel Popplewell at Somerset. He set himself a goal, and vowed that if he had not been picked for England after so many years in the game, he would quit. He wasn't, so he has. It would have been easier – and much less frustrating – if you had not been picked for England so young, and had left the game at the same age as Popplewell. You would have gone straight into a successful and fulfilling life, without all the terrible problems you have had from cricket.' Edmonds mused on that one, and added: 'I expect if I had never gone to play county cricket, I would now be pretty well established as a property magnate. But as it is, I'm a cricketer who does a bit of business on the side.'

Edmonds spent his first term at Cambridge basically cruising around and seeing what was going on. He also unintentionally offended the rugby fraternity, which couldn't understand why a man who had played for England Schools was unwilling to commit himself fully to university rugby. But by the beginning of the second term he was already involved in cricket. A notice had been pinned to a board inviting would-be university players to assemble for a trial: Edmonds signed on and went to the indoor nets at Hatfield.

Perhaps there was a little colonial defensiveness in the way he did not over-commit himself to the rugby boys. And indeed, after his experiences of school cricket, he was wary of playing sport with stuck-up, semi-competent Poms. However, the captain of Cambridge did not match this description at all: he was a man named Majid Khan.

Sport has a certain kind of snobbery that tends only to come into play at a certain level of the game concerned. At the low 'fun' levels of every game, incompetence is tolerated: reputation, personal contacts, and ability to put on various kinds of good show all count for a great deal. School sport thrives on such things. But at higher reaches of competence, this vague notion of acceptance of one's colleagues for themselves peters out, and the sportsman's snobbery – the conspiracy of excellence – takes over. To be a man of talent is enough. To be a great guy and to lack talent is to be an outsider, to be locked from the conspiracy of the talented.

Edmonds had been driven mad at school by the vast gap of ability between himself and the semi-competent, if amiable, Poms he had played with. But as soon as he joined the practice sessions with Cambridge he was content: these guys could play. They were part of the elite. Edmonds relaxed and joined them. Their ability was enough to win his respect – his own ability had the same effect on his colleagues. At last, he was among like-minded sportsmen, men who were, like him, in love with the pursuit of excellence. Edmonds also had the advantage of the advice of Cyril Coote, the coach and groundsman: 'A marvellous old boy, who helped and encouraged me all the way.' As a further plus, Majid Khan, a cricketer by any standards of exceptional ability, was in charge: a few years older than the rest, vastly more experienced at cricket, and overwhelmingly talented. There are few people of whom Edmonds talks with more respect and affection than Majid: and it was under Majid's captaincy that Edmonds turned himself into a truly formidable and fulfilled cricketer.

Edmonds said: 'I remember ringing Majid for the first time, and saying: Hi, I'm from Zambia, and I want to come and play. He said: fair enough, great. So I went along to Hatfield and had these nets on perfect batting strips, and just smacked the ball around all over the place – it was easy. I looked really good. Before the season started, we had a meeting at Majid's house, and he said: look, I want you to open the batting. So I thought, well, what an extremely good ploy that is.

'I knew at the time that Majid didn't want any slow bowlers in the side. University spinners are generally useless. What we needed, if we were to get anywhere at all against the counties, was a strong batting side, and bowlers who could do a restricting job. So I was a batsman, and when we came to our outdoor nets, I was still looking good. When you rate yourself and others rate you, and you are batting number one, you have a completely different mental attitude to when you come in number nine or ten. One way or another, you tend to live up to your batting position.

'But all this time, I was still rating myself as a topline bowler. And in the nets, I bowled as I would do anyway, and it was obvious I could bowl. So I was then considered to be an all-rounder.'

Edmonds played his first first-class match against Warwickshire, and did nothing. But his second, against Leicestershire, was different. Many cricketers have found their first appearance alongside real cricketers, with journalists and knowledgeable old heads looking on, to be an unnerving experience. But Edmonds, riding the up escalator, did not find it so. He took nine wickets, in fact, and Leicestershire promptly asked if he was interested in joining them. It was the start of a pattern: Edmonds kept bowling well, and counties kept asking him to join them. 'Majid and I had a chat, and he said: "Obviously all these counties will keep coming for you." I said yes, it looked like it. So he told me that the best thing to do was to get it all out of the way – and to sign for Glamorgan, for whom he just happened to be playing in the long vac.'

There was something about Glamorgan, however, that didn't really ring the bell for Edmonds. The county didn't seem to him to contain the essence of all that English cricket has to offer. He wanted the finest backdrop in the world for his cricketing talents, and somehow, Wales did not seem to be the place that would provide it.

But Edmonds did not find all this competition for his signature unsettling: quite the reverse. He enjoyed his cricket immensely, revelling in the conspiracy of talent. He was playing in an excellent team, packed with men of obvious ability. Some of these pursued first class cricket later on: some had talents that faded, others had no intention of playing the game at a higher level: one team-mate was not only a medic, but a man whose religious convictions meant that he refused to play on Sundays; others had career aspirations that ruled out first class cricket later on – but who were determined to make a go of it in their few years at the university. At Cambridge, Edmonds played alongside Majid Khan; John Spencer, later with Sussex; Dudley Owen-Thomas, later with Surrey; Robert Hadley, who joined Glamorgan; Keith Steele and Chilton Taylor who both went on to play first class cricket in New Zealand. This was a real cricket team, and Edmonds, at the heart of it, revelled in playing real cricket at last.

Edmonds found his respect for his colleagues matched by amazement at the standard of full-time county cricketers. He could not believe that men who had been playing the game seven days a week for years were not better: 'I saw these guys play, and I felt like John McEnroe: you cannot be serious! I couldn't believe that these guys were earning a living playing cricket.' Edmonds at once had their measure. So many university spin bowlers get found out when they come to bowl on what are, in comparison with school and club pitches, perfect for the batsman. County batsmen find such spinners totally innocuous: cannon fodder. Hundreds of these poor little apprentices of spin have retired hurt after some cynical county batsman has happily seized the opportunity to restore a flagging first class average at his expense. But anyone who treated Edmonds unceremoniously came grandly unstuck: 'I was full of the arrogance of youth. There wasn't a single batsman I didn't think I could get out – and that attitude helps you with every ball you bowl.'

In a ridiculously short time, Edmonds had become the mainstay of the Cambridge attack, and was regularly bowling 40 overs an innings. He had dropped down the order to number seven as a result, but he was the number one bowler: for Edmonds, there is no happier position to be in. And the counties were racing each other to sign up this prodigious talent. 'We went to Glamorgan, and this very nice guy, Bill Edwards, who was their chairman at the time, asked me to have a talk with him. He took me to his car, and started telling me about how much fun it was at Glamorgan, and how all they needed to be a really good side was one slow left-armer, and I'm not trying to pressurise you, Phil, but do you mind signing these forms I've got right here? So I said, don't worry, Bill, I don't feel pressurised at all, and do you mind if I don't sign these forms?'

Kent also took a serious look at Edmonds, the more serious since he had been to school there. Warwickshire, Leicestershire, Glamorgan and Middlesex were also full of anxiety to get the name of Edmonds onto their books. But it was inevitable that Edmonds would go to Middlesex. Where else would he go? Some people seek the chance to be at least a medium-sized fish in any small pond, but for Edmonds, the best was barely good enough. Not that Middlesex were the county the others all had to beat at that stage: they were going through a transitional period, though Edmonds quite accurately read a thrusting determination to put the county at the top in their young and ruthless captain, Mike Brearley. But it was not just the county, and their hopes of top-dogmanship, that attracted Edmonds to Middlesex. It was the cricket ground that they rent from the Marylebone Cricket Club: Lord's.

'If I was going to play cricket seriously, then I wanted to play for England, and it seemed to me that there was a consistent bias in favour of players from the home counties. I don't know if this applies especially to Middlesex, but when I considered who to sign for, I had in my mind's eye the big press box above the Warner Stand. It would be far easier to play for England by doing well at Lord's, than it would be doing well miles away in Glamorgan. Majid always used to tell me about a fellow named Alan Jones who was one of the finest opening bats in the country for years. He played for Glamorgan: and he got to play in just one Test match, against the Rest of the World. He made nought and one, and even that got taken away from him when Wisden decided that it wasn't an official Test match after all.'

No, it had to be Lord's for Edmonds, and so he chose Middlesex unhesitatingly. Partly there were the Machiavellian reasons of the political realist: the bank of press seats, the proximity of the England selectors, and the traditional home counties bias. But there were also romantic reasons: Lord's is, undeniably, Lord's. For Edmonds it was the only place to be. And there were the considerations of his career outside cricket: he wanted to become involved as soon as possible in business, and for him, business meant London. 'There were many things that kept me at Middlesex during the really bad days, when I couldn't get into the Test side, and my captain at Middlesex didn't think I could bowl,' Edmonds said. 'But one of the reasons that I stayed was that I could not see myself playing away from Lord's.'

When Edmonds joined Middlesex, he did not join a great team. They had a talented captain who was eager to have his own way, but in those days, Brearley was not considered to be the finest captain that ever drew breath. To be a highly rated captain, you need first of all a highly talented side. At the time, Middlesex were about halfway there. But by signing up young, and eminently talented young cricketers like Edmonds, Middlesex were preparing themselves for their future assault on cricket's major trophies.

And for Edmonds, it all began well. He is not the kind of cricketer that can give a ball-by-ball commentary of matches that are long gone. He can hardly remember a set of bowling figures: the details of his performances and his opponents blur. He cannot even tell you who he played against when he first played for Middlesex. In fact, he played against Essex, and took five wickets in the match. He signed for Middlesex on a match contract worth the dizzying sum of £30 a game, so far as he can recall – even these figures do not stick in the mind. But he is essentially a pragmatic and forward-thinking person. But when he finally joined the Middlesex staff after he had left Cambridge, he asked – and got – £2,000 a year, rather more than some of the senior pros were getting. That opened the way for a complete restructuring of the salaries the county paid.

He may have forgotten the exact pay he received for his first appearance for Middlesex, but the effect the summer had on Edmonds' life was unforgettable. He was straight into the top class: playing cricket for money, and being taken seriously as a top bowler for the future. He was playing in the county championship, a great step upwards – and yet again, he found the transition dead easy. The up escalator carried him onwards once again. 'I just bowled. I believed I was capable of getting anybody out, and so I just bowled – and got wickets.' In five matches, he took 14 wickets for Middlesex that first summer. True, the Thames didn't spontaneously combust at this entrance into Lord's, but for a boy of 20, it was a fine start, more than merely promising. By the time he had returned to his studies at Cambridge the following autumn, he was clearly on the path that would lead to selection for England, provided that his precocious talent did not blow up on him. Edmonds took it all comfortably in his stride. He was wholly unsurprised that his entrance into first class cricket had been so comfortable. Naturally he would consolidate his efforts and play for England. Even at this age, his total confidence, his self-trust, was amazing. It is a quality that some can find alarming. Edmonds certainly has, largely unintentionally, alienated many people, and others have been secretly frightened by these qualities. Edmonds is not a man who resists the temptation to go one-up on anybody – particularly if the fellow is a batsman.

In his second year, Edmonds played rather more rugby at Cambridge. But there were a number of immediate problems. His height, weight, strength and aggression made him a natural No 8 – but the Cambridge captain, Gerry Redmond, was a No 8. Edmonds was therefore shunted about, often playing at centre, because he had pace as well as everything else. But it was not his best position, and he felt a little restless: Edmonds likes to give of his best and shine, or do nothing at all. He doesn't care to make up the numbers. He did, at least, have the ineffable pleasure of flattening Gerald Davies in a college match.

But Edmonds' involvement with Cambridge rugby was never heartfelt, though he represented Cambridge several times. The university squad were going through a period of fitness fanaticism: 'It was all about seven mile runs and train, train, train. I remember saying: look, we can *play* seven days a week. We should be super-fit anyway. Our strength should be that we are young and enjoy playing. We should concentrate on throwing the ball around, speed to the ball and elusive running – because men's sides are always going to beat us when it comes to weight and strength. Our advantage is that we can enjoy ourselves. But no, we had to make the game into a penance, and the training into something worse: train, train, train. And then we would go out and play big sides, and the players would be saying: "Christ, it's London Welsh – how can we possibly play them?" What an immature mental attitude!

'So in the end, I packed the game in. I went and played golf instead. I remember one coach telling me I was crazy, he said I was one of the best No 8 he'd ever seen. But there it was, I was fed-up with the whole set-up. It was stupid, in retrospect. I've seen guys like Mike Biggar, not particularly talented, but amazingly determined – so determined that he got to captain Scotland. Because guys with determination succeed, don't they? But I lost my determination to succeed at rugby. If I had kept it, I believe I could have gone on to play for England. But I didn't. I didn't even get a blue. I did all the training and stuff at school without a thought, because it was virtually part of the curriculum. But at university you have freedom for the first time. If I'd been forced to play rugby, I would have been a good player. But I had my chance, and I just didn't want to take it.'

Of course, a spell at university is generally an intoxicating time – often literally. But it is freedom that goes to people's heads. Anything else is just a bonus, if a highly acceptable one. Though in fact, Edmonds has never been a great carouser. His principle memories of Cambridge are not of riotous times. His work interested him, and he did it well, without becoming fanatically studious. The cricket took huge slices of his time. 'But apart from that, my most vivid recollections of Cambridge are of wasted time,' he said. 'Drinking coffee in the Turk's Head, and talking. Sure, I had a good time, but I could have done so much more. There were brilliant men lecturing every day, but it was always so much easier to mess around having a "good time". Let's have another cup of coffee, or let's go and listen to Carole King records.'

There is a sense in which the point of being at university is the opportunity to waste time: accustoming oneself to freedom, discussing the meaning of life until four in the morning and often coming up with the answer, with optional Carole King records in the background. These are some of the grander things that any university can offer the undergraduate, who sways his way perilously across the tightrope between boyhood and adulthood. But Edmonds does not agree with such a notion of university life. He cannot believe that he did not take more of Cambridge's vast opportunities for self-improvement and self-advancement. Cricket was the one area in which Edmonds positively advanced his cause. Vast acres of the rest of his time, in his opinion, he wasted.

It was an interesting period in which to have time to waste. The first years of the seventies saw the era of hip studenthood at their peak: Edmonds himself then had a spectacular mane of real blond hair that tumbled well past his collar. Many other students saw the meaning of life in political idealism. 'There was a lot of talk about Daniel Cohn-Bendit and so on – though I was always surprised at the naïveté of the so-called radical guys. They wouldn't even listen to my suggestion that Tariq Ali could be an agent provocateur, reporting back to the establishment, for example. Admittedly there was a heroin addict along the corridor from me, but mostly, I was struck by the reactionary attitude of the students.' Whether this says more about Cambridge or about Edmonds I cannot say. Certainly, hipsters and politicos were not known for their attendance at the cricket. But the freedom, which Edmonds feels in retrospect he had too much of, was something others revelled in. Edmonds mildly despises the way in which he enjoyed himself so much at Cambridge, and had so little to show for it.

Frances Edmonds might dispute the validity of this statement. After all, Edmonds met her at Cambridge, and later married her. To meet the woman of one's dreams at Cambridge! They must, one assumes, have had many an idyllic moment in that ridiculously beautiful setting: the grandiose architecture, the river and the willows, the punting, the sun and the freedom and above all, the feeling, that every Oxbridge student always has, that life is quietly waiting until you can be bothered to seize it by the scruff of the neck and make a glorious success of it. 'The one thing that I can remember about punting along the river is the time that Frances laid me out with a punt pole,' said Edmonds. 'I've never been so annoyed in my life. She gave me the most terrible crack. She insisted on punting herself, of course, since she wanted to be the star of the show – '

Frances understandably interrupted this: 'The reason I was punting was because you couldn't punt. Being left-handed as well as incompetent, you just went round in circles.'

Edmonds insists that he was, without question, 'the punt king'. But if so, he was lying back on his throne, because Frances was punting, and, at the same time, singing one of the songs that gondoliers sing when they pole you around Venice: 'Sa-an-ta-ah Lu-oo-ci-ee-ah!', she carolled, and accidentally walloped Edmonds on the back of the head with the business end of the punt pole. 'I could cheerfully have thrown her in the river.'

Clearly, then, this was a match made in heaven. A match in the sporting as well as the other sense of the word. To be a third person in their conversation today can at times give one the dizzying sensation of being an umpire at Wimbledon. The teasing, the banter and the outright arguments are part of the pattern of their life: both revel in confrontation.

When they met, Frances was a star student in modern languages. She also ran the Italian Society, which she did gorgeously and lavishly, and ran the society into an enormous debt. She now works in the fiendishly difficult field of interpreting polyglot conferences.

Much of her work is with the European parliament. She 'has a whiplash turn of phrase in several languages', Matthew Engel wrote in *The Guardian*. The principal of these are French, Italian and Spanish: also English. She is quite recklessly funny: she it was who described Paul Allott as 'a Botham clone, only slimmer and brighter. Who isn't?'

This appeared in the notorious piece she wrote for the *Daily Express*: in the same one she summed up Graham Gooch: 'Plays cricket rather well.' She also wrote of Edmonds: 'Works very hard at trying to be controversial and an iconoclast, but basically a pillar of the establishment.'

It was typical of Edmonds that he greeted this with a smile and a shrug: when his team-mates complained to him, he referred them to his wife, she being manifestly capable of taking responsibility for her own actions. Cricketing wives tend to be squaws, who live through their husbands' achievements, and who sometimes show an unladylike glee at the failure of their husbands' professional rivals. But Frances has got her own act together, thanks, and is capable of being as awesome as P. H. Edmonds – and as awkward – when she wishes.

The subject of Frances came up when Edmonds appeared on Wogan, who asked if, after all the hoohah about the *Daily Express* piece, would she be accompanying him to the West Indies? 'I hope so,' he said, smiling contentedly at the camera, 'because I'm very much in love with her.' Which would probably provoke Frances into calling him a crawler. They are a pair of exceptional people, and you would expect their relationship to have its own rules.

Their relationship flourished at Cambridge, and indeed, everything about the pair of them flourished. Frances achieved a degree of tedious excellence, and Edmonds marched on triumphantly in his cricket career. He had the spectacular advantage of being able to compare the standard county pros he bowled to with Majid Khan, and this was a comparison that few county batsmen could live with. Everything about playing cricket for Cambridge gave Edmonds vast encouragement: including his accession to the Cambridge captaincy in his last year. 'I loved being captain,' he said. 'As you know, I get bored easily. It is old hat to say this, I know, but as a captain you are hardly ever bored. You are involved all the time. Even today, I find my concentration wavering, when I am batting or bowling, so I bowl bad balls or get out to some innocuous bowler. But when you're in charge, the adrenalin never stops flowing. That is the situation that brings the best out in me.'

Tim Lamb, now Middlesex secretary, was on the opposite side to Edmonds in the Oxford-Cambridge match in which Edmonds was captain. 'He had star quality,' Lamb remembers. 'His confidence was quite clear from his demeanour. It was partly physical, but partly it was something else about him. People were somehow always respectful towards him. He was very much a man who knew where he was at. Even as a student, he was a person people would look up to.'

At that period, Oxford-Cambridge matches were terrible, drawn-out, attritional affairs, rather like India-Pakistan Test matches: matches which it is nice to win, but for the love of God, you mustn't lose them. Lamb, a bowler, recollects blocking Edmonds out for half an hour at a crucial stage when Oxford were batting for time. 'I even cracked a full toss of his for four, which was something of an achievement for me, since he had absolutely dominated the match,' Lamb said. Oxford crucially gained the time they needed, and Cambridge's attempted slog for victory cost them quick wickets, and so they too settled for a draw.

Edmonds left Cambridge after three years with a fair degree and an awesome cricket record. He moved straight to Middlesex and became a full-time cricketer. Here, his attitude to the county pros change subtly. 'I still didn't rate them alongside people like Majid. But at the same time, I couldn't help but be impressed by their canniness. They might look to me as if they couldn't bat: but all the same, year after year, they'd be getting their thousand runs.

'So I respected that kind of ability. And I grew to understand the terrible insecurity of the professional cricketer. The awful jealousies that come from the insecurities. The way cricketers – and especially their wives – check through the figures in the paper, hoping that their rivals have had a bad day. It is a horrible, negative approach to the game: but when you think that these guys' entire livelihoods depend on these figures, it is easy to understand. The thing about cricket is that everyone can read what you've done in the paper the next day. You can't bumble along like a guy in an office: everyone can see exactly what you've achieved. So it is inevitable that people start to look over their shoulders at the other players.

'This is an attitude that I have never shared. Call it arrogant, if you like, but what matters to me are my own abilities. I want to be the best because of what I can do – not because of the failings of a load of other people.'

It is a crucial difference in attitude between the top class player and the middle-ranker: especially in cricket, where the very essence of the game is confrontation. It was the same sense of being a natural winner that saw Edmonds begin his involvement in business. Being nobody's fool, it was not long before he had a measure of success: it rapidly became clear to everyone at Middlesex that he was a man of the world to whom success came naturally. The sweat and toil – the need to climb cliffs with one's teeth – that most people associate with money-making and achievement did not seem to apply to Edmonds. His self-belief does not permit the kind of insecurity that makes it necessary to check on people's results and achievements: he is totally secure in himself where such matters are concerned. He is mistrustful, or insecure if you prefer, in other areas. His feelings about the way the world works make him suspicious of the establishment's aims and motives. Hypocrisy and expediency is a favourite phrase when referring to the establishment or establishments.

But as he embarked on his life as a full-time cricketer, there was no need to feel insecure on the cricketing front. In his first full season with Middlesex, he took 77 first class wickets. The press box above the Warner Stand duly saluted his emergence as one of the finest slow bowlers in the country. One day, they wrote, this man must play for England – one day soon. And next season, he did. Not every one, however, was pleased.

CHAPTER 4

THE ALLY

There are certain people whose fate seems to be interlocked with one's own. There seems to be no particular reason for it, but lives overlap, interweave, in patterns of friendship, emnity, power, ambition, conflict and conspiracy. There is no element of choice in this. Kurt Vonnegut's crazy mystic, Bokonon, in the book *Cat's Cradle*, claims that this is a mystical phenomenon. Bokonon says that throughout the world there are teams of people mystically linked to do God's will: he calls such a group a karass. 'If you find your life tangled up in somebody else's life for no very logical reason, that person may be a member of your karass.' The concept of the karass is explained in 'Bokonon's Fifty-third Calypso':

> Oh a sleeping drunkard
> Up in Central Park
> And a lion-hunter
> In the jungle dark,
> And a Chinese dentist
> And a British queen –
> All fit together
> In the same machine.
> Nice, nice, very nice;
> Nice, nice, very nice;
> Nice, nice, very nice –
> So many different people
> In the same device.

The fates of two unquestionably different people, Mike Brearley and Phil Edmonds, seem to have been deliberately intertwined by a malign, mischievous and twisted godling. If karasses really exist, then Edmonds and Brearley are in the same one. Perhaps some one should have told them that there was no point in resisting the mystic force of the karass. It would have saved them both a lot of trouble. But as things transpired, their cricketing fortunes remain somehow linked. As one cricketer waxed, the other waned: the position changing until the other cricketer waxed, seemingly at the other's expense. Now things have changed once again: with Brearley in retirement, Edmonds has waxed as never before.

Brearley was in his first season as captain of Middlesex when Edmonds breezed in from Cambridge to play in the long vac. Brearley was to remain in charge of Middlesex until 1982, by which time he had become the most celebrated purveyor of the art of pure captaincy in the history of the game. As captain of England and as moulder of the Middlesex success machine, Brearley became a legend for shrewdness, tactical acumen, brilliant handling of temperamental players, the man who could bring the best out of every one, and the man who acquired his person cliche: 'He's got a degree in people'. 'Rodney Hogg was the man who said it first,' Edmonds said. 'So it must be true.' When Brearley left the game, he put the final gloss on his reputation at the great guru of leadership with his book, *The Art of Captaincy*. The book was rapturously received: my colleague at *The Times*, David Miller, summing up the Brearley myth as he wrote: 'The most perceptive book ever likely to be written on cricket captaincy.'

In one of Edmonds' benefit promotions, a kind of kids' sports magazine (an interesting collector's item that includes many pictures of Edmonds with hair), he includes the de rigeur questionnaire:

> Favourite car: a sponsored one
> Favourite food: steak and chips
> Biggest influence on career: Mike Brearley

Had Edmonds known at the start just how big an influence Brearley was to have on his career, and on his life, he might have charged headlong into the city and made his pile in the property market a long time ago. However, not being gifted with second sight (and sometimes apparently not even gifted with first sight), he became a full-time cricketer. He won his county cap in his first full season. His entry into cricket was inevitable, rather than the product of a clearly thought-out decision. In fact, Frances thought it was just something he was going to do for a couple of years 'to get it out of his system' before he settled down to do something serious. At the same time, he set himself up with some serious work to do in the winter: he joined a firm of chartered surveyors for whom he could work in the winter, acquire an RICS qualification and gain experience in the property market. Edmonds said: 'My degree in land economy gave me exemption from the professional exams of the RICS. In view of my natural bent towards property, it seemed the natural thing to do.'

However, he left the firm after the second winter, through force of circumstance and the opportunity to further his cricket career with a tour overseas. It is a decision he still sometimes questions. He remained in cricket, for cricket manifestly refused to leave his system, and looking back at the worst of times – and there were many and they lasted a long time – he cannot believe that he remained in cricket. 'I must have been insane.' But cricket had him hooked with a devastatingly powerful and addictive combination of factors. Firstly it provided him with an outlet for excellence: who can ever give up something at which they excel, and excel publicly? And secondly, cricket provided him with an unending series of frustrations. Frustrations are also hard to relinquish: you keep thinking that next day/next week/next match/next season, it will all be different, everything will fall into place, that it is just a question of hanging on in there a little bit longer. And in all this, Brearley was inextricably involved.

At first, though, it seemed that all the hard thought Edmonds had given the question of which county to join was paying off. Quite apart from all the tempting reasons that had tipped the balance, there was the bonus that Middlesex had an ambitious Cambridge man as captain. What more natural than that a bright new ambitious Cambridge boy like Edmonds would get on with him? And initially they got on well. 'I liked him, I liked the fact that he was such a talented cricketer,' Brearley said. 'I enjoyed his company, and we had dinner together often. We talked a lot, and argued a lot. His company was always very stimulating. He was refreshing, and I liked his views on cricket even when I didn't agree with them.'

Indeed, Edmonds had much to do with various famous incidents that demonstrate Brearley's own unconventional side. Edmonds loves to make things happen, try things out, to get one up on an opponent. Brearley shares Edmonds' belief in the need to grasp the initiative. Edmonds' one-upmanship makes him a mickey-taker of the most challenging kind, with a love of mischief-making and of the unconventional. It was partly because of his influence that Brearley demonstrated, with great élan, his own pleasure in eccentric captaincy.

Brearley mentions with great glee in his book that when batsmen have solidly and apparently inescapably gained the initiative he has, as a desperate, last resort, put himself on to bowl 'moon balls' – extremely high, under-arm full tosses designed to land from a dizzy height onto the top of the bails. In fact, he started this enchanting ploy after talking it over with Edmonds, asking him if he thought it was ever a good idea to bowl 'your really bad bowlers'. Edmonds gave an instant encouragement: 'Why don't you bowl moon balls?' 'You can embarrass a batsman out,' Edmonds said. 'Not to hit a really bad bowler for hundreds of runs looks like incompetence, but getting out to such a bowler looks even worse. The batsman gets caught between his obligation to slog and his fear of getting out.' He is caught, in fact, 'like a cat in an adage', as Bertie Wooster would say. The fact that it was the England captain bowling these mad loops made them the more intimidating, and added to the chance that they might just make something happen.

Making something happen is what it is all about, of course. 'There is no doubt,' Edmonds says, 'that Brearley was a very good captain. Things did happen when he was in charge. Because he was always wanting to do something to ensure that they did.'

It was in pursuit of this philosophy that Brearley was delighted to go along with Edmonds' notion of placing the fielder's helmet at short mid-wicket. To hit the helmet (when there is no fielder inside it) is to score five runs, and Edmonds wanted to tempt a pair of extremely dogged – perhaps boring is the word I am looking for – Surrey batsmen into error. He thought the target worth five runs might tempt the batsman into pushing a little across the line. 'It reminded me of playing in the garden in Zambia, with buckets for fielders,' Edmonds said. Perhaps inevitably, the batsmen didn't want to play, but it is nice to see such unconventional notions being given a whirl, good to see a captain going along with a bowler's whims, good to see talented, original cricket minds in harmony. As Edmonds said, there is too much seriousness in cricket. And in fact, the incident led to a change in the laws of cricket (other sports have rules: cricket has laws). A helmet can now only be placed directly behind the wicket-keeper.

There is, however, a certain mentality that finds all new ideas, and all new people in cricket, a personal affront – or a threat if you prefer. This is the mentality of the old pro types, the seen-it-all, done-it-all boys who annually nudge and nurdle their way to the required number of runs or trundle out the decent tally of wickets. These fellows are not the sort that get on with bright young boys from Cambridge.

We have, over the past ten years, got used to the Middlesex success machine: to seeing them as the Liverpool of county cricket. We forget that at the beginning of the seventies they were not exactly world beaters. The side was in a state of transition. There was youth at the helm, a clique of 'wily old pros', and a whole bunch of promising sprogs coming through. Indeed, the foundation of the Middlesex success was being laid while Middlesex was heaving about in the throes of change: the under-25 side were carrying all before them in their own competition.

Brearley said: 'In the 1960s, the Middlesex side was divided between the stars who had played many times for England, many of whom were household names, people who had been my heroes, in fact, when I was at school – players like Fred Titmus, Peter Parfitt, John Murray, Eric Russell, John Price. By the time I was captain, there was an uneasy situation between them and the rest of the staff . . . the rest were not considered equals. Though I could see that my job was to bring these people together, it wasn't always an easy thing to do. I had some difficult times personally, as captain. I wanted to avoid hostility, and I didn't always feel wanted.'

This was not paranoia: this was the real thing. He wasn't wanted, not by the old pro contingent, not when they were at their most hostile. Brearley added that 'at a time when I was least secure in myself', Edmonds was a great help. Edmonds epitomised the youthful Middlesex thrust for future honours: Middlesex were beaten finalists in both knock-out finals in 1975, and won the championship in 1976 to set the era of success in full motion. Edmonds always appeared as massively confident, and, indeed, mostly was genuinely confident. He always felt he was capable of turning the ball past the bat of any august player round the county circuit, always wanted to bowl the ball that would turn the greatest names in cricket inside out. And on his days, he did so. He played with the old pros on level terms right from the start, and found the ease with which he did so risible: 'You cannot be serious!' Daily rubbing shoulders with the great men around the counties did not mellow or humble Edmonds. He was a vastly encouraging man for an ambitious, upcoming captain to have in his side.

Edmonds had the added asset of drawing some of the fire from the old pros. 'They resented the fact that cricket came so easily to him – and yet he had absolutely no *need* to be good at the game,' Tim Lamb, the Middlesex secretary and former playing colleague, said. Old pros desperately need to gather their quota of runs or wickets to remain gainfully employed until the dread day of retirement cannot be deferred any longer. But Edmonds strolled in, looking and behaving as if he owned the place, casually took dozens of wickets, 'and yet it was patently clear that he could also achieve far more off the pitch than any one else. There was always a degree of friction between him and the rest under the surface.'

Edmonds recalls these difficult times for Brearley, and talks with some amusement about the help he gave Brearley at the time. 'My behaviour then was a great source of enjoyment to Brears. Particularly with regard to old pros like John Murray. Now J. T. was obviously a great keeper in his time, but by the time I arrived, the physical edge of his greatness had been blunted a little. But his self-image was timelocked in the period of his former glory. I never heard him apologise for dropping a catch. He was always very smooth, very elegant, immaculately dressed: all image. Tap the gloves, tap the hat, big circle of the arms, wait for me, chaps, right, now I am ready, you can bowl now. Crouch down, drop the catch, pick it up, throw it back to the bowler – all elegance! Never said anything to the bowler, never said whoops, sorry, I dropped it. And I used to be fielding at, say, cover, with Brears at mid-off, and I'd be making remarks like "Well, catch the bloody ball then!" Brears would hear, and he was very much on the same side. I was his boy, he was feeling exactly the same kind of impatience.'

Brearley is at pains to point out that he was also able to traffic with the old guard, and shies at the term 'allies' used to describe his then relationship with Edmonds. 'I don't see it in those global terms,' he said. However, the division between old and new players certainly existed, and the friendship between Brearley and Edmonds was also a fact of life. And one by one, the pros left the side, with Peter Parfitt, in particular, holding regrets for some years that he had left the side so early. By 1976, Brearley had a side of men who had come up with him, and which strolled off with the championship. Edmonds said: 'Brearley is one of the hardest and most ruthless men I have ever met. It was that strength of character that saw him through that difficult period.'

Edmonds was one of the stars of the new breed of Middlesex men. He made the transition into full time county cricket with quite ridiculous ease. You did not need to be gifted with extra-sensory perception to see that the boy was a promising player: certainly he would play for England. Probably be a regular for years. That bank of pressmen above the Warner Stand saw Edmonds coming, and duly took note.

At this time, no one without second sight could have predicted the future apotheosis of Brearley. Though he appeared to be a good captain, he had periods of struggle with the bat. In fact, in terms of playing success, there was a sense in which the captain was being upstaged by the newcomer from Cambridge.

Edmonds was a youth still touched by gold in 1975. He was selected for England for the first time – in point of fact he was an England player before Brearley. The old pros held a dressing-room sweep-stake on the number of runs he would make in his first innings for England. Mike Smith (whom Edmonds remembers as probably the best exponent of dressing-room humour he has known) went to great pains to buy up what he was convinced was the lucky ticket: number nought. Edmonds spoiled his fun by scoring 13 not out.

He also was not wholly unremarkable as a bowler. In fact, he had one of the most glorious Test match debuts any bowler has ever had. He went to Headingley to play against the Australians, and in his first 12 overs for England, he took five wickets for 17 runs.

You might uncharitably have expected that Edmonds' reaction to this immense achievement would be an outbreak of swagger that reached unprecedented levels of arrogance. It was not. He was embarrassed. He felt he had bowled dreadfully.

THE ALLY

For once his ball-by-ball recollections are fairly vivid: Edmonds had the gift of almost total amnesia about the little details of most matches he has played in, unlike most top sportsmen who recall every aspect of every great day, from how many eggs they started with to how many pints they finished with. Edmonds said: 'I came onto bowl, and I didn't think too much about it. But I bowled two or three reasonable overs. Then I tried a quicker ball, and it was a really bad ball. A long-hop. It kept low; Ian Chappell went to smash it through mid-wicket, and lo and behold, he was bowled,' said Edmonds, breaking into sheer poetry at the memory. 'It was a perfect example of what coaches say in the nets: any straight ball has a certain lethal quality. Chappell went off and slammed the door. I think it was Ross Edwards next, and the very next ball I bowled, he padded up. It was a perfectly ordinary ball, it drifted in with the breeze, it wasn't an arm ball, but I get a lot of in-drift naturally, more than most, and Edwards didn't expect it perhaps. He padded up, for no apparent reason, to a ball that would have hit middle and off: very good appeal, thank you very much, that's two.' A hat-trick would have been too much, perhaps. But the luck continued. 'I got Greg Chappell with a leg stump half-volley. Apparently he had just been asking Tony Greig (the captain) whether he had deliberately moved Underwood from long leg to just behind square. "Is that where you want Unders?" he asked. Greigy said nothing. Then Chappell swept the ball like a rocket straight to Unders and was caught. "That's where I want him," Greigy said. Max Walker I did get with a good ball – orthodox turn, caught at slip.' The other victim was Doug Walters, leg-before.

Frances remembers: 'I was at my parents at the time, and I had never seen a Test match, and wasn't much interested. I was just drifting about, arranging things in the garden, while my brothers were going wild. I remember meeting Phil at the train station that evening, and all the people kept coming up to him and shaking his hand.' As soon as he and Frances got to the sanctuary of the car, Edmonds told her what had happened that day. 'I have never bowled such a load of shit and taken so many wickets in my life!'

'I was embarrassed,' Edmonds said, and he is not a man much given to embarrassment, least of all where his own success is concerned. 'I believed that wickets should be a due reward for performance. It was Fred Titmus who told me that was ridiculous.

"How many times are you going to bowl brilliantly and not take any wickets?" he said. And he was dead right. You bowl brilliantly all day, and you get 1 for 110.' Bad balls take wickets even if Brearley only ever took one with moon balls. In the 1985 Ashes series, there was a long period in which Edmonds and Emburey were bowling beautifully, establishing total control. But not a wicket fell. On came Ian Botham, and bowled two successive long hops. The second of these gave Botham a wicket. 'C'est la vie,' said Edmonds. C'est la cricket, anyway.

The second innings bowling performance in Edmonds' first Test match put the five wicket haul into a better perspective. Edmonds took 1 for 64. Greig had one of his manic periods of all-out attack, and Edmonds bowled to Doug Walters with a cluster round the bat and no one out square on the off. 'I remember saying to Greigy, are you sure about this? This is my first Test match, and he is one of the finest cutters in the game. If I'm a fraction short, I'm going to get clobbered. I bowled some bad balls, and got carted.'

But naturally, after that first innings, Edmonds was selected to play at The Oval, on what used to be a typical Oval strip: flat, flat, and getting flatter. 'I didn't bowl well and Ian Chappell swept me to buggery,' he said. Ah well. It was still perfectly clear that Edmonds was a major find. Obviously, he was certain to go the winter tour.

There was one problem. There was no winter tour. It is quite staggering to think that such a state of affairs should exist: but international cricket has not always been the non-stop machine it is now. In fact, in the winter of 1975–76, it was South Africa's turn, but the D'Oliveira affair had already happened, and there was no question of going there. So there was no tour at all.

Edmonds went on a tour of South Africa by himself. He played for Eastern Province: as an ambitious young cricketer, it seemed to make sense for him not to lose the rhythm. He did well. 'Playing for Eastern Province was tremendous,' he said, 'particularly as I had the privilege of playing with Graeme Pollock, who must surely be one of the great players of all time. As a team, we did extremely well. We won their 60-over knock-out contest and came second in the Currie Cup. In many ways, I found their whole cricket atmosphere much healthier than England's. Most of the cricketers were amateurs, who were building up careers outside cricket. Secondly, there was none of the treadmill syndrome of English county cricket. We

44

played only eight or ten first class matches in the season, so there was a tremendous build-up to every match. Each one was almost like a Test match. It was impossible to become blasé, as people do in English county cricket. In England, standards are often affected by the "well, there is always tomorrow" attitude.'

Edmonds struck up a friendship with an Eastern Province colleague, a hulking great Afrikaaner named Etien Schmidt. Schmidt was the butt of most of the dressing-room jokes at the time, he was meant to be the thicko who didn't speak English. The rest of the team found it baffling that a man with a Cambridge education should pick out Schmidt as his particular mate. Edmonds found the South African snobbisms – the way in which the 'English' South Africans look down on the 'Dutch' – unsympathetic.

He and Schmidt, in true Edmonds entrepreneurial style, set up a business together – as, so Frances insists, rag and bone men. Edmonds had gone out to South Africa with an agreement that he would be given work in a financial institution, thus combining education in both cricket and real life in a satisfactory way. But the job was not what Edmonds had hoped and besides, by this time the entrepreneurial blood was flowing strong in the Edmonds veins. He and Schmidt got themselves involved in the buying and selling of rags – the motor-car business used a huge quantity of rags before paper rolls replaced them. Edmonds and Schmidt did rather well from the adventure, with Edmonds putting on the smooth, polished Englishman bit to sell to big companies, and Schmidt doing the rough diamond act round the small mechanics shops. It was a similar double act to that of the Edmonds brothers, Pierre and Phil. Thus the friendship prospered.

Edmonds also played a fair amount of cricket in South Africa with a team called the International Wanderers, which included Ian and Greg Chappell, Dennis Lillee, Max Walker and Ashley Mallett, among other notable cricketers. He enjoyed the rousing atmosphere created by people who shared his colonial upbringing: the tough trading of insult on the field, which can be quickly forgotten as soon as play has ended – the same attitude that Edmonds learnt at his school boxing matches, 'fight it out and forget it' – and which he searched for in vain in England. In England he was to learn that emnities are more bitter and more personal matters that can last, apparently, for years.

The winter had a lasting effect on Edmonds' cricket career. It was his moment in spotlight as the bright and promising newcomer: but there was no tour in which he could maintain the high profile of a great young cricketer in form. Even as he was selling rags and having a good time, his brilliant start as an international cricketer was slipping away. By next summer, back in England, Edmonds was no longer a name on everybody's lips, and Greig was not looking too hard for spinners. The West Indies were coming, and Greig believed that pace was the way to make them grovel. As famous last words go, those remarks of Greig's on his intention to make the West Indians grovel have an unforgettable quality. South Africans are justly famous for their tactful approach to the sensibilities of black people. (Indeed, I recall watching one of the one-day matches which in those days took place after the Test matches, at Lord's. Greig's decision to field near the boundary where I sat was greeted with a great bay of pleasure by my neighbour: 'Who's grav'lin' now, you lang streak of peace?')

The grovel series was also remarkable for a quite spectacular piece of bad diplomacy from Edmonds, and one which cost him dear. He was picked to play in the final Test of the series, at The Oval. At the time, he had a split spinning finger: the most tiresome and irritating injury a spin bowler can suffer from. A flayed area of skin you could cover with a postage stamp puts an entire body out of action. Edmonds, the new boy, was anxious to give of his best, and knew that on the flat Oval wicket, against the West Indies, a spinner might have to bowl for two days at a stretch. He knew that he was not up to that: he pulled out.

'I knew I had a responsibility to tell the selectors about it,' he said. 'It would have been criminal to have played and then not been able to bowl at 100 per cent. I was very much in two minds, but in the end I did the honourable thing and told both my county captain and the chairman of the selectors on the Tuesday before the Test.'

He explained the nature of his injury, and said he was perfectly capable of bowling short spells on the less demanding county circuit. Inactivity is always irksome to Edmonds: he won permission to play for his county at Chelmsford while the Test match was going on. It seemed the sensible thing to do.

But it looked a quite extraordinary thing to do. 'Looking back,

THE ALLY

I cannot believe that I was so naïve, or that no one advised me of the implications,' Edmonds said. And people wondered: did he, perhaps, lack the stomach for international cricket? Was he, with Machiavellian cunning, dodging the risk of getting carted by Richards and Co? Was it decided then that Edmonds was not really the sort of chap required for England cricket? Whatever the reasons, Edmonds was not picked for the winter tour of India, and had he gone, there is absolutely no doubt in his mind, or in the mind of any sober observer, that he would have established himself once and for all as one of the country's finest spin bowlers.

For India made a hideous mistake. They prepared a series of raging turners, and completely overdid it. At the time, India had the greatest spin bowlers in the world, but in trying to suit them, they overspiced the curry. Edmonds describes their tactics: 'They had no seam bowler, so apparently Gavaskar would open the bowling by running down the wicket scraping it with his studs. He used to wear extra long studs. Then the spinners would come on. But they made the mistake of preparing bad wickets, and our seamers as well as our spinners could exploit them.'

Underwood went out, and had a lovely time – with 29 Test wickets he was the top bowler. (There is no actual rule stating that you cannot take two slow left armers on tour, and indeed, Edmonds played his first Test match alongside Underwood. They are completely different bowlers.) Underwood said, in a newspaper piece of the time, that the person he felt most sorry for was Edmonds. Indeed, to gorge himself on spinners' wickets would have set him up for the next few years. But through bad luck and worse judgement, Edmonds missed out.

It was the first tour when Edmonds' omission was amazing – but there were to be plenty more of those. Edmonds had, after all, in the 1976 season, been picked for a Test match, scored 892 first class runs and taken 88 first class wickets. As seasons go, that one just about passes muster. And yet Edmonds missed out.

His captain, Brearley, went. And Edmonds stayed at home.

Brearley was now on the up escalator, while Edmonds – who nurtured ambitions of captaining England – was going the other way. Also, the friendship between the two of them was beginning to show signs of wear. The two cricketers who had shared frustrations at the clique of old pros, were no longer allies. In fact, the relationship between them on the field was beginning to turn sour. It was eventually to turn sour beyond all measure.

If Edmonds had known that he was to spend the next eight years of his life in seething frustration and thwarted ambition, he might have thrown his cricket whites out the window, put on a suit, gone charging down to the City in pursuit of a few million. But without extra-sensory perception, and victim of optimism, the incurable disease from which all sportsmen suffer, he believed it would all be better – next match/next month/next season. Wrong, wasn't he?

And his fate and his frustrations over the next eight years were all hopelessly entangled with the fate and the success of Brearley. Edmonds may not have had second sight, but he met a mysterious old man at Lord's who apparently did. It was during Edmonds' last season at Cambridge, 1973. The old man approached Edmonds and said: 'You mustn't join Middlesex.'

Edmonds had been loving it at Middlesex, getting on really well with Brearley, and was startled by this. 'Why not?' he asked.

'You won't get on with Mike Brearley. You will never fulfil yourself at Middlesex.'

'Of course, I poo-pooed it at the time,' Edmonds said. 'But I never forgot it. I never saw the old boy again.'

CHAPTER 5

SNAKE BALLS

People talk about 'slow bowlers with fast bowlers' temperaments' as if this were a bizarre phenomenon. In truth there are a lot of fast bowlers who do not have fast bowlers' temperaments, and a good number of spinners who are fiery, aggressive, ultra-competitive and mortally aggrieved each time the ball passes the bat without taking a wicket. Tony Lock is a classic example. So is Phil Edmonds. 'The more slowly I bowl, the more aggressive I need to be, and the more strength and the more body I need to put into each delivery,' he said.

The comic strip notion of the spin bowler is the fat kid with glasses and a vague, benevolent expression, who can make the ball sing the Hallelujah Chorus. It doesn't apply to Edmonds. He sees spin bowling as a task for a strong man with a strong mind: a matter that is romantic, beautiful, and spectacular. While he admires Bishen Bedi's ability to shuffle in, applaud boundaries struck off his bowling, and generally charm, in every sense of the word, his opponents out, Edmonds knows that such wiles are not his. He approaches spin bowling with the nature of a swashbuckler, he sees bowling as a matter of grace, style, class and controlled aggression.

I remember trying to draw Edmonds out on the technicalities of spin bowling with the question: 'What is your stock ball?' Edmonds replied: 'Mentally, my stock ball pitches leg and hits off.' The reply sums up Edmonds' approach to cricket: he is not generally trying

49

to winkle and weasel a batsman out: he is not basically seeking to tie down, to frustrate and to bore his man to a dismissal. He aims to turn a batsman inside out with a ball that turns somersaults.

This constant optimism, aggression and self-belief are Edmonds' great strengths as a bowler – and have also been on occasions, his weaknesses. His restless seeking for wickets was one of the many things that made Bob Willis, when he was captain of England, uneasy about Edmonds. Willis once said that the art of captaincy comprises having better fast bowlers than your opposite number, which is one of those remarks that says a great deal more about the speaker than it does about the subject. 'I would want Edmonds to bowl a string of maidens to give the seamers a rest, to bowl to a tight field and to stop the scoring while the seamers had a blow,' Willis said. 'But that was not what happened. I would put Edmonds on and he would be bowling three different kinds of deliveries in an over.'

'I don't really have the mentality to plug away offside, offside, offside,' Edmonds said. 'I might be a lot better off if I did. Indeed, in India on the 1984–85 tour, it was essential to bowl long, tight spells, and I bowled hundreds of maidens. But normally, the old-timers come along and say, you should have been bowling to a 6–3 offside field, saving the singles, and there might be a lot of truth in what they say. But I'm not sure I really have the temperament for it as a long-term strategy. It's not in my personality to bowl that way. I can remember one match against Northants, though, on a slow wicket with nothing happening and I thought: all right. I'll try it the old-fashioned way. I'll bowl off-stump to a 6–3 field. And I did, right through the match, and I got Allan Lamb twice. On a hard wicket, he would have crucified me, down the wicket and over the top, but on a slow wicket he couldn't do it. And I frustrated him out twice over. But normally I find it difficult to contain my aggression like that. I can't say to the batsman: you're going to make a mistake. I say: I'm going to get you out.' There is a world of difference in the two approaches.

Mike Brearley is critical of Edmonds' mental approach to bowling. 'He hasn't made the best use of his abilities,' he said. 'He might attribute that to me – I attribute it to him. He hasn't learnt enough. He often bowls worse to ordinary players. John Emburey is different: better on green wickets, a good nibbler of the ball. He is not as capable of bowling the really good ball that gets top players out on good wickets, and on a real spinners' wicket he is unlikely to get the results Phil would. But Phil is always trying to attack – and often you want a bowler to be defensive.' But David Gower attributes much of his success in India to Edmonds' restrictive, mean-spirited bowling.

Allan Border, on the losing end of a Test series with Edmonds and Emburey bowling against him, said: 'It is the fact that Edmonds and Emburey bowl in tandem that makes them so dangerous. One spins in, one spins out. Emburey is playing a waiting game, while Edmonds is attacking you with every ball.'

The man who certainly knows Edmonds best as a bowler is Paul Downton, who has kept wicket to Edmonds for countless overs for both Middlesex and England. 'He has had real problems keeping to me, as well,' Edmonds said, and this is something with which Downton will – cautiously – agree. Downton said: 'His mental attitude when bowling means that he will not normally settle for containment. This can make him very exciting, but it is also a flaw. He wants every ball to be a magic ball. For this reason, he is even harder to keep to than Derek Underwood – and I have kept to Derek on wet wickets when I was with Kent. Derek will normally be content to contain and pressurise a batsman, but Phil hardly ever will. To make things even more difficult for a keeper, he bowls a much fuller length than most bowlers – two feet to a yard further up than Emburey. He is trying to attack, and so he bowls fractionally short of driving length all the time. The ball is a yard closer, which is an enormous distance if the ball does anything unexpected. It is especially hard if the batsman is tempted into an attacking stroke, and all the flurry blocks your vision, and you can't see what unexpected thing the ball has done.'

The point is that big spinners of the ball like Edmonds can turn the ball so much that they beat absolutely everything. A ball that turns sideways is spectacular, but it doesn't always take wickets. But when the ball is pitched further up, and then turns sharply, the batsman has a crucially diminished time in which to adjust – while the ball has every chance of finding gap or edge or pad. It is tough for batsmen – and a nightmare for keepers, who must take a sharply turning ball obscured by the batsman round about their shins. Because the ball is pitched up so high, a keeper standing up must take the ball a good way before it is at the top of the bounce. The natural place to stand to keep to Edmonds is a couple of yards back, but that, of course, is not on, for it would give the batsman the chance to amble up the wicket and play golf shots without fear of a stumping.

Downton continued: 'Edmonds uses his strength with every ball – he has a magnificent action and a really strong arm. He could have been a great pitcher in baseball.' Edmonds, incidentally, goes along with that, and said, with characteristic restraint: 'I could have been the finest pitcher in the world, man.' Admittedly his tongue was not far from his cheek at the time.

As a cricketer he bowls a potent curve ball which would stand him in good stead if he translated it into baseball terms. Downton elaborated: 'He bowls with a natural curve, a drift into leg, so much so that on occasion he is almost unplayable on a *flat* wicket.' Edmonds said: 'For years, I always wanted a wide leg slip for the ball that drifts in with the arm. However, the tiny percentage of chances actually taken there finally persuaded me to abandon the tactic.' Downton again: 'He has an enormous range of deliveries. He bowls with a big action, so close to the stumps that there is no hint of roundarm. He is completely side on. But on the other hand, he lacks Underwood's consistent accuracy, and could not do what Derek does. Because he attacks so hard, he will go for runs as well as take wickets.'

Downton finds keeping to Edmonds enthralling: perhaps the biggest test in cricket. But there is one part of Edmonds' cricket that enrages him. Edmonds likes the blood to run fairly hot when he is bowling. He is baffled and furious when a good ball fails to take a wicket. He finds it especially exasperating when he senses that a batsman will charge him, adjusts his length accordingly, finds the batsman charging – and then adjusting his stroke to pat the ball back defensively. Downton said: 'When that happens, he will sometimes pick the ball up and hurl it at the stumps, generally give away four runs, and then yell at me for not catching it. I remember on one occasion he threw the ball the far side of the batsman, and I thought: I'm not going to poke my head round the corner and catch the ball with my face. Let him give away four runs. But 99 per cent of the time, we get on well on the cricket field.' In fact most cricketers will say exactly the same about most other cricketers:

that 99 per cent of the time they get on fine, and you have to ignore the other one per cent. That is how team games work.

Edmonds concedes – with quite gentlemanly resignation – that criticisms levelled at him for over-attacking are justified. He even accepts with resignation some barbed comment from Robin Marlar in the pages of *The Sunday Times*, who upbraided him for this failing during the summer of 1985. This is not a failing in his cricketing brain – it is the nature of the man. 'It is undoubtedly true that there have been times when I have been a trifle inflexible in my thinking – particularly about wanting men at bat-pad and short leg. If there is even the remotest semblance of a chance of a bat-pad catch, I like to have a man there, on occasions when it might be better to tempt the batsman into big, booming drives, with an extra man in the covers for the catch – exactly as Robin says.' But Edmonds conceding runs through quixotic attempts to take a wicket is the price you must pay for Edmonds bowling the magic ball that gets the opposition's best player out. If you want the one, you must make the best of the other. If the Edmonds style isn't working, you take him out of the attack: this is true of every bowler, and it is a lesson David Gower appeared to have learnt as regards Edmonds, and Botham too, in that '85 Ashes series. But in the previous tour of India, Edmonds became the number one bowler, and found no mental problem in bowling with all the meanness a captain could wish for.

Edmonds always bowls better when appreciated by his colleagues and his captain – as anybody might. His natural penchant for attack tended to become counter-productive under Brearley, when Edmonds eventually became the fifth choice bowler for Middlesex. 'I used to get annoyed when I knew I should be bowling, but in a way that made me over-aggressive when the wicket didn't warrant it. And so I'd end up not bowling as well as I might, and I'd get taken off.'

On the whole, Edmonds finds a certain kind of anger a great asset when he is bowling. Brearley once got thoroughly up his nose in a Test match against New Zealand at The Oval, and Edmonds responded by bowling Bev Congdon, the captain, with his stock ball, the one that pitches leg and hits off. ('I was annoyed by some particularly prissy comment, and that had a remarkably positive effect on the next couple of balls,' Edmonds said. He continued: 'When I'm not angry, I tend to get bored. Boredom is my biggest problem as a cricketer. I get bored even when I'm bowling. When I haven't got something like anger to focus my attention, my mind does wander, and I'm bowling a bad ball. And for no reason at all, I'll be thinking: I dunno, maybe I'll toss this one up a bit and maybe it'll bounce a bit and maybe he'll get caught . . . I'm not really concentrating. Often I think I'm concentrating, but I'm not, I'm going through the motions and, whack, I've gone for four runs, and I'm thinking: how did I manage to bowl that terrible ball? But when I'm angry, I'm concentrating on everything that's happening, and every single ball is going where I want it to. I'm much more in control.

'It was like that when I bowled against Australia at Lord's (in the 1985 series). I was still angry with Border after a brush we had had when I was batting, and that helped me bowl extremely competitively that morning.' Indeed, it was quite a spell: Australia needed a handful of runs to win, but with memories of Headingley 1981 on their minds, they stumbled to 65 for 5. Botham had been expected to provide the main threat, but he was upstaged by Edmonds, bowling into Craig McDermott's footmarks. He lured Kepler Wessels into an unbalanced forward lunge, and Gower ran him out from silly point – a virtual stumping, as Matthew Engel wrote in the *Guardian*, even if the bowler doesn't get any credit. He then got Dave Boon with a beauty that turned a mile and a half, and, as a bonus, picked up Wayne Phillips with a ridiculously good catch off Emburey. Australia scrambled home in the end – England needed to have scored another 50 runs to trouble them – but Edmonds had proved his worth as an England man in his first Test on English soil since he was called back into the side. And anger had helped considerably.

These were ideal circumstances for Edmonds to bowl in: on song, appreciated by all around him, getting batsmen in trouble, and with a clear short-term aim in mind – get 'em out by lunch or lose the Test. This close mental horizon is something that traditionally galvanises quick bowlers: Bob Willis at Headingley in 1981 was a classic example: Wayne Daniel bowling in the championship against Leicestershire in the 1985 season was another. But even with the scent of victory in his nostrils, Edmonds' mind can go walkabout. While Botham cannot wait to earn eternal glory for himself by knocking down nine, ten and jack, something in the Edmonds mind stops him going for the jugular when the victims are easy ones. 'I can see myself letting off the pressure at the time. I say to myself, come on, bowl your best, concentrate, you can get two or three easy wickets – but something in me stops me from delivering the goods.' In his heart, Edmonds scorns easy victims. For him, cricket is about getting great men out with great balls. He is by nature a duellist: a man in love with confrontation who relishes an opponent worthy of his mettle. Bamboozling the no-hopers does not excite him. 'Well, statistically it does,' he said. 'So much of cricket is judged by statistics, and nine, ten and jack count the same as Allan Border and Ian Botham. My statistics are not as good as they should be because I don't get the easy wickets I ought to.'

For Edmonds, bowling is an emotional matter, into which he must pour his strength, his will, his anger and his concentration if he is to make things happen in a worthwhile way. Accordingly, he must have a worthwhile opponent at the other end, a worthwhile foil for the duelling side of his nature. Confrontation is a joy to him: in conversation he is an arguer. If you spoil things by agreeing with him, he is likely to start bowling conversational chinamen and arguing from the opposite point of view. Unsympathetic captains and colleagues find him oppositional: it is the same part of his nature that makes him wish to take on the opposition's best player and argue him out, to bowl him a case that is proof against all counter-argument. His summer-long duel with Allan Border was one of the highlights of the 1985 season, and it finished with the results a crucial 55–45 in Edmonds' favour. On the county circuit his boredom vanishes when the great players walk into the middle: 'Bowling at Botham brings the best from me. I love it. I've got him out a few times, and he has now reached the stage when he doesn't really want to get out to me again. If he takes it into his mind to have a slog, he is a good enough player, because he's so correct technically, to get away with it. And on these occasions, I would assume that he is impossible to bowl to. But I'm currently at the stage when I have got him out a couple of times caught and bowled, which is an especially annoying way to get out, off a mistimed drive, that sort of thing. And so he is at the stage when he doesn't want to let go fully against me. If he did, it might be a different story. In the same way, if Border had got away with slogging me early in the series, he could well have hit me to all parts afterwards. But he didn't. And though he did exceptionally well, it was always with due respect to what was happening. He couldn't ever quite cut loose.

'I loved bowling against Border. But I find it very difficult to just bowl, bowl, bowl, to build up pressure on a batsman and bore him out. Even when I was bowling 40 overs an innings at Cambridge, I can't remember having the mentality that says: you're not going to score a run off me. I was always thinking: I'm going to get you out, and I'll just try this one . . .'

Like your classic fast bowler, Edmonds seeks wickets rather than maidens. But a fast bowler is trying to blast an opponent: Edmonds is seeking to master him. He is not the devious type of spinner that wants to sneak a ball past with its slippers on: he wants a ball that gives him booming, dramatic proof that he has the mastery. He wants a batsman beaten all ends up. He does not complete his sumptuous action with an equally gorgeous follow-through: his unstoppable reaction is to halt, straddle-legged, monarch of all he surveys, defying the ball not to turn square, hands raised in readiness for the appeal or the caught-and-bowled chance, and an expression of amazement flitting over his features if, by some miracle, the ball does not take a wicket.

Edmonds began as a quick bowler, or at least, as a pre-pubescent purveyor of pace and fire. He did not start spinning the ball until he was in his early teens. 'I think all spinners should, for technical reasons, start off as seamers,' he said. 'You need a strong body before you can bowl spin. It doesn't matter what people say. When you see little kids of nine trying to spin the ball, you can see it is a nonsense. I don't know a top-line spin bowler who has not bowled seam at one time – Titmus, Illingworth, Laker, Embers, me – I changed early, but I was already mature physically. I was a quick bowler for Lusaka junior school, and I did loads of bowling to my big brothers in the nets at the time. We would be out there practising every afternoon. Since I was bowling to 18 year olds when I was 12, my quick stuff wasn't all that dynamic, but bowling three, four, five hours a day, I certainly learnt to put the ball on the spot.

'But I bowled so much in the nets that my hand would start to get tired. And so my hand would no longer be right behind the ball, which is a must if you want to bowl fast. The wrist and the hand are important to get right for a fast bowler. Every now and then, Wayne Daniel will bowl a ball when his hand is not right, and it will generally loop gently down the leg side. In the nets in Zambia, I became a bit lazy in this area, bowling with my hand slightly to the side of the ball, and so I found myself bowling naturally in a style that was a little like Derek Underwood's. From there, it was a very short step to separating the fingers and trying to spin the ball.' Edmonds had large hands even then, which made the transition a simple one. Indeed, Frances blesses the day when Edmonds decided not to do medicine at Cambridge. She is convinced that as a surgeon his hands would make him a corpse-maker supreme – though Edmonds says in his defence that he was 'extremely delicate with the old scalpel' in dissection classes.

The sight of a classic cricket duel, especially one between spinner and top class batsman, is an enthralling one. It is also especially frustrating. The tension, the drama – and Edmonds is a theatrical player – come billowing over the boundary ropes in waves. But even with binoculars trained on every ball, the details themselves are not easy to unravel. 'It is a hard thing to explain,' Edmonds said. 'People imagine you have a certain number of different balls in your repertoire, and you bowl them one by one in ways you think will get the batsman out. But it is nowhere near as clear-cut as that. It is much more to do with feel, with very slight variations. I don't have an armoury with a certain number of deliveries – I have an infinite number of tiny variations. You make the variations in tune with what you feel is happening with the batsman. You will feel the pressure building up as the duel is on. The batsman will be in trouble, and won't be able to score, and hardly any batsman is relaxed when he is not scoring. And you are trying to anticipate the way in which the batsman will play. With experience it becomes not easy exactly, but you can switch into a general way of thinking that is anticipating what the guy will do next. You try to combat this, maybe with the arm ball, maybe a fraction slower than before, or maybe you toss one high but a bit short, hoping he will come down the wicket at you. If you get it wrong – if he senses what you are doing – he will lay back and cut the hell out of you. And Fred Trueman will say what a terrible ball. What it is, is that the batsman has out-thought you. If you get it right – as I did when I had Allan

Border stumped at Old Trafford – there is no argument from anyone.'

Edmonds is constantly trying to persuade a batsman to expect one kind of delivery and then confound him with another. It is a game like paper-scissors-stone, a matter of bluff and counter-bluff, one in which a superior ability to read minds separates winner from loser. But in Edmonds' game, there are far more than three options: a touch more bounce, a smidgeon more turn, a little shorter or a little fuller, a fractional change of line, a suggestion of fizz and jump . . . that is what the confrontations are all about, and winning them is what makes Edmonds revel in cricket.

'I used to get especially annoyed with Brears when I would anticipate a batsman hitting over the top, and tell him I wanted a man out. Brears would refuse, and tell me to keep the man saving the one. Lo and behold, four runs over my head, and I'd be furious.'

Lateral movement in the air is part of any spin bowler's stock in trade, with the left-armers arm ball slicing in to the right-hander. Edmonds bowls with an immense amount of natural drift: 'My natural ball curves into the right-hander almost like the bias on a wood in bowls. It drifts and dips in and then spins away if the wicket is receptive – it is another reason why wicket-keepers find it hard to keep to me. Embers (John Emburey) gets drift too, but with him it drifts away from the right-hander, into the keeper's line of sight. With me the ball gets hidden behind the batsmen, and then it spins.

'I remember playing under Tony Lewis in the MCC match, and I kept drifting the ball down the leg side into the breeze. Lewis said this could not be happening – the breeze should be blowing it to off. He wouldn't accept it, but it was happening. I think the seam must have been acting almost like an aerofoil, that some aerodynamic principle was making it bite into the wind.

'Alternatively, it could have happened because there was something wrong with my hand. There are so many things that affect spin bowling. And there are so many things that can go wrong, for that reason. I remember the first match Embers played for Middlesex, I was turning the ball square, and Embers could not turn it an inch. I think he was spinning the ball, but, possibly because he was nervous, he wasn't landing the ball on the seam. His wrist was slightly wrong, and he was undercutting the ball. It was landing on the polished face of the ball and so it was not biting, just going straight on.

'For me, a lot depends on what it is that you are visualising happening at the other end. Often you are visualising yourself doing something that is not technically possible. I often visualise myself bowling what I call the spitting cobra ball – the ball on a length that leaps up and hits the splice and gets caught at silly point. It is a slower ball, and I put a lot of effort, a lot of strength, a lot of *body* into it. I visualise it as a vicious top-spinner, like a Bjorn Borg forehand, but I don't think this is actually what I am bowling. It is not technically possible for a finger-spinner to bowl top-spin, despite what Richie Benaud says. To do that you would need either a double jointed wrist or a bent elbow. But all the same, I sometimes get the ball to spit and bounce. Perhaps it is in the rip of the arm, I don't know, but the old snake ball gets wickets all right.'

For Edmonds, these duels are not grim, vicious, grinding struggles. They are flamboyant explosions of single combat: Captain Blood on the beach with whirling rapier and have-at-you-now. He bowls as a D'Artagnan of cricket. Mentally he is always ready to swing across the room on a chandelier. No wonder Willis got irritated when he asked Edmonds to bowl maidens. Equally understandably, Gower, with Emburey at hand to purvey any amount of attritional off-spin and to bowl as many maidens as one could wish for, can cheerfully throw the ball to Edmonds and wait for him to rip things up a little and apply the kind of pressure that only the fear of being out every other ball can bring. Such is Edmonds' nature, and it is the antithesis of the wily old pro ideal: an ideal based on a canny looking after of number one, a self-promoting mastery of the craft, meanness, and an ultra-professional approach to the notion of competition. Edmonds, however, can be charged with unprofessionalism, though one could equally well see it as a throwback to the age of the golden amateur. The old amateur spirit lives on in Edmonds' approach to cricket. It is not that he would ever refuse a sou that was his due for playing the game, but the cash is no more than a highly acceptable bonus for him. The fact that he can make money readily outside the game means that cricket can be precisely that for him: a game. He reckons he lost the chance to do a million pound deal by going on the tour to India: when you are duelling in seven figure sums in the City, it is understandable that duelling in a cricket match can be approached in a more cheerful and ebullient fashion. There is, perhaps, a romantic streak in Edmonds. When I suggested this, he burst out laughing and so did Frances – but he is a cavalier and not a roundhead when it comes to playing cricket. Perhaps it was a romantic approach to playing cricket that kept him in the game during the long black period under Brearley.

A romantic, or at least a whimsical nature shows in his love of bowling chinamen. At one time he would willingly seize opportunities to bowl his half-controlled wrist-spinners, and when Middlesex were bowling for a declaration he would enjoy himself hugely. Of course, he would bowl two lousy balls every over, so that was eight runs gone for a start, but he could get the odd ball to leap and fizz, and Edmonds could never resist giving it a crack when invited. But he doesn't do so any more. He has concurred with the roundhead views of the old pro bowlers, that it is not their job to give away runs. It all goes down on the analysis under the name of P. H. Edmonds. To his lasting regret, you cannot signal the scorer that you wish to have the following overs recorded under another name, or as 'Edmonds (but only messing about)'. If it says 9-0–60-0 in the papers the next day, absent selectors will snort and say, Edmonds, damned inconsistent fellow. So that particular piece of quixotry has been, reluctantly, abandoned. But there are plenty of others: his batting, for example – and his fielding.

But it would be hopelessly wrong to conclude from any of these suggestions of the amateur spirit that Edmonds does not care. He cares desperately, especially about the big games. People tend to see Edmonds' aloofness and arrogance and conclude that he must therefore possess a mind untouched by doubt: a man so self-assured that he can carry on inviolate in any self-determined course he is set on – he doesn't care.

Such a notion is a grave error. No one who did not care most desperately could suffer from the most dreadful of sportsmen's mental afflictions – 'the yips'. 'The yips' is a golfing term which is specifically used to describe putting failure: a famous victim of the yips was Bernhard Langer, who was once prone to three-putts from two feet. But the yips – a breakdown in elementary technique – afflicts the practitioners of every sport. Snooker players get 'the snatches' when the all-important cue action degenerates into a panicky stab; tennis players get a destructive stiffness in the crucial joint and call the affliction 'the elbow'; darts players get a comic failing called 'the sticks' when they are unable to release the dart and let it flop pathetically onto the floor; soccer penalty takers hit the corner flag; rugby place kickers kick the ball all along the ground; and spin bowlers suffer from all kinds of weird manifestations of the yips. Spin bowling is both complex and precise, and the smallest breakdown in co-ordination, in the rhythm and sequence of the movements of delivery, can lead to dreadful, humiliating failure. Such repeated failures finished poor Fred Swarbrook of Derbyshire, a slow left-armer who could bowl beautifully in the nets, but out in the middle sent the ball soaring over the batsman's head. It happened after many years as a wily old pro: and he never did put it right: the yips destroyed his career.

It is a dreadful, a frightening thing to happen. Edmonds, perhaps understandably, does not care to go into deep self-analysis on the subject. 'There was a time, for a few weeks early in 1980 and again in 1981 when I certainly could not bowl a hoop down a hill. I was having a hard time with Middlesex. I was Brearley's fifth choice bowler, and that really got to me. Bowling became a nightmare. The only remedy was to get into the middle and bowl as much as possible. This is what I did. I remember bowling 50 overs in a single innings in a second team game against Essex.

'The mind can play weird tricks on you. During the tour of India (1984–85) I lost my run-up completely. I suppose the reason was an over-anxiety to succeed. My run-up became so extraordinary that Chris Cowdrey nicknamed me "The Croupier", because I was always shuffling. I have seen Ray East, Don Wilson and Norman Gifford, all slow left-armers, suffer from the same sort of problem, in different degrees, but I could not believe it was happening to me. It seemed quite extraordinary not to be able to accomplish a simple thing like running up smoothly from five paces. Actually, the affliction was even beneficial in one respect. I became solely concerned about what was happening at the batsman's end. Also, the lack of momentum generated by a smooth run-up made it essential for me to compensate by exaggerating my follow-through, so that I would really be bowling, as opposed to just putting it there.'

It was an affliction that could have been a disaster. But Edmonds was not going to let any mental aberration destroy his final chance. He shuffled up to the wicket, to gales of hearty laughter from the crowd, and bowled. It helped that he is strong enough to bowl off one pace – almost like a baseball pitcher, in fact. Paul Downton said: 'He was a *huge* factor in our win. We were wary of him at first, but he was as good as gold. He had a huge confidence in his ability, and became the number one wicket taker on the tour. The man we looked to any time we badly needed a breakthrough. He loves to be the number one guy, and he helped people and talked generously throughout the tour.'

He got through the problem thanks to his deep-seated belief that his ability could not be an evanescent thing. For the sake of his own self-esteem, he needed to be great, and thus the yips were defeated and he became the number one. It takes more steel to have the yips and recover, than never to have had the yips at all. And to move from the yips to the position of number one bowler in a victorious touring side – that takes some doing.

CHAPTER 6

CHANEL NO 5

Mike Brearley has the most enviable reputation in cricket. He is the master of captaincy, the lovable intellectual who hums cello solos when batting against Dennis Lillee, the man who wins Test matches from impossible situations, and who personally created Ian Botham. He is the most respected judge in English cricket. His shrewdness, fairness, tactical acumen, and above all his ability to handle players, his 'degree in people' have made him a legend of brilliant leadership.

He nothing common did, or mean, so the legend goes. Edmonds is tempted to describe Brearley in other terms. When he was asked to fill in a questionnaire at the World Championship of Cricket in Australia, he had to state what he considered his biggest break in cricket. Edmonds wrote unhesitatingly, 'the retirement of Mike Brearley'.

The two men had started out as the very best of colleagues, but amiability and mutual regard was gradually and inexorably replaced by suspicion and the erosion of mutual esteem. And this went on for years, years in which Edmonds failed to command a regular England place and which saw his reputation as the most impossible cricketer in England grow apace. The relationship degenerated so drastically that the two were prepared to have a fist-fight in the pavilion at Perth during the lunch interval of a Test match.

The different reputations of Brearley and of Edmonds ensure that public sympathies will immediately be with Brearley, and against Edmonds. But in fact, Brearley says the near punch-up was mostly his fault. This violent shouting match was only stopped from turning into an all-out fight by the intervention of John Lever. Nor was the row unexpected. It was simply the most obvious symptom of the disease that had poisoned their relationship for a long time.

Such is Brearley's reputation that one tends to think that any one who cannot get on with Brearley must be pretty weird. Indeed, Edmonds *is* pretty weird. But if he is a weirdo, Brearley is another. Brearley is as singular a man as is Edmonds. Both are set apart from the crowd by their intelligence, and by their natural aloofness. Both can repel invaders with the most chilling air of self-sufficiency. Brearley is a strange man, and one with the defensive reactions of a hedgehog: save that Brearley has rather more prickles. And while he may have a degree in people, he was unable to captain Edmonds in a way that brought the best from him. 'I certainly found Edmonds the most difficult player I have ever had to captain,' he said. And an England captain naturally wants to work with the tools that suit him best.

Edmonds would argue, though, that the England captain should simply work with the best tools available, and that he should have been an automatic selection for England for years. But instead, Edmonds was left out time and again, while his reputation for perverseness – some of it earned, some it not – grew and grew. Even after Brearley retired as England, and then as Middlesex captain (three retirements, all told), Edmonds remained outside the pale. He tends to put this down to the Brearley legacy of mistrust: subsequent captains Botham and Willis were Brearley disciples, and probably the better players because of that. Brearley could neither manage nor trust Edmonds, therefore Edmonds was seen as unmanageable and untrustworthy: a reputation David Gower ignored – and profited considerably by ignoring.

Towards the end of the pre-Gower era, Edmonds was given a number of last chances, always with the unwritten clause in his contract that half-an-inch out of line and he would be out again. Edmonds, with his wild, perverse streak, generally obliged. Thus people became, if this is possible, increasingly wary of him.

Brearley and Edmonds look back on the long years of rift with a degree of puzzlement now. Each has a natural tendency to blame the other, along with a more civilised tendency to shoulder a small part of the blame himself. Each will admit that the years of niggling strife and occasional forays into overt hostility have left a bitter aftertaste.

Of course, the word 'bitter' is not one permissible for sportsmen. It has acquired a special meaning in the sporty world: about once a year, every sportsman gets asked if he is 'bitter' about being dropped or whatever, on the understanding that he will instantly deny it: 'No, Brian, I'm not bitter about it; I'm disappointed, obviously, but I realise I've just got to buckle down and work at me game and, well, Brian, I just hope I'll be out there with the lads for the final.' The one thing a sportsman never admits to being is bitter.

Edmonds, however, admits that in certain moods he does feel bitter that the better part of his cricketing life was wasted, and that the better part of his cricket life was so unprofitably entangled with one man. Musing over old memories, old rows and old frustrations, is a desperately unhealthy pastime, and that is exactly what I was forcing Edmonds to do throughout our many long sessions with the tape recorder. 'I know I sound bitter sometimes on these tapes,' Edmonds said after one such meeting. 'But I don't normally spend my evenings thinking about the rows I had with Mike Brearley. In business, I'm always excited about the deal I'm trying to do next week, not wondering about the one that fell through the week before. In the same way, I don't spend much time worrying about my wasted years as a cricketer. Now I am deemed to be an acceptable part of the England set-up, there is no point in doing anything except being absolutely positive, and looking to the next series, and aiming to take a lot of wickets.

'And yet,' he mused, 'how is it that nowadays I am regarded as a reasonably good international bowler – and that in Brearley's day, I was fifth choice for Middlesex – so much so that they used to nickname me Chanel No 5? I haven't changed, nor have my abilities.'

Brearley says that Edmonds was the most difficult man he ever had to captain, but the difficulties cannot all be laid at Edmonds' door, nor would Brearley seriously wish it so. The truth of the matter was that their relationship was a cosmic mismatch. However, this begs a question: was it Brearley that Edmonds had a problem with? Or just captains? 'Who has he not been a mismatch with?' Brearley asked, betraying a wee smidgeon of bitterness himself.

In fact, there are at least two England captains with whom Edmonds has got on rather well. In a strange sort of way, his relationship with Gower has been wholly satisfactory to both men, and has resulted in Edmonds playing a leading part in winning two series. Another captain Edmonds has worked well with has been Geoff Boycott, of all people. If you were looking for proof that Edmonds is an oddball, you need look no further.

Brearley acknowledges this in *The Art of Captaincy*: '(Edmonds) felt, I think rightly, that he would have done better, with his own Zambian upbringing, with a more extrovert, abrasive and physically tough captain, like Ian Chappell. Possibly Geoff Boycott got more out of him than I could. I noticed that Edmonds reacted well to Boycott's jibes in the nets. Each time he bowled a bad ball, Boycott would leer at him, saying, "Another fower!"' Edmonds goes along with Brearley's interpretation. Both he and Boycott value plain-speaking, and each rates the other highly as a cricketer. Harsh criticisms each make of the other are based on a bedrock of immense respect – even liking. Boycott has gone to the extent of calling them 'the Fitzwilliam boys' – Edmonds was at Fitzwilliam college, Cambridge, and Boycott is from Fitzwilliam in Yorkshire.

Boycott became captain of England on the 1977–78 tour of Pakistan and New Zealand after Brearley got his arm broken by Sikander Bhakt, and had to go home. Edmonds was on the tour. 'I hadn't been getting on too well with Brears. I felt ambivalent about his departure,' he said. 'Everyone was saying what a terrible captain Boyks was. All I know is that when Brearley was in Pakistan I didn't do much, and when Boycott took over, I got 7 for 66 at Karachi in the third Test.' Being respected by your captain, and being given the ball by your captain tend to make for better bowling performances from any one.

Boycott's captaincy is mostly remembered for his part in one of the most peculiar Test matches of recent years. It was at Christ-church, New Zealand. Edmonds said: 'Boycott had been having a bit of a nightmare with the bat, and was averaging about 13. He was getting more and more agitated by this. He was thinking more about his own involvement than the team situation, and this got worse at Christchurch. We had batted extremely well, and when they replied, it looked as if we would be able to enforce the follow-on. They had a late order stand, however, and it began to look as if we would have to bat again after all. The more likely this looked, the more agitated Boyks became. Then we had to bat, and I remember Brian Rose saying to him before they both went out to open: "I suppose we're going to go out and slog it?" Because we needed to hit a quick hundred, and leave them needing 300 on a baddish wicket on the last day. Boyks said: "You play it your way, and I'll play mine." And it turned out to be one of those instances when Boycott, normally very adept at giving away the strike early on, found himself unable to do that. After six overs, Rose had hardly faced a ball, and the score was 6 for 0, when it should have been 30 for 1. Rose got out having a slog, and then Randall was run out backing up – no warning, just thank you very much. I remember saying in the papers that had we done that at school, the master would have taken us in and flogged us, and quite right too.

'So then Botham went in out of turn to hurry things up. His version of what happened next is that he played out to short extra cover and called for a run that wasn't there. Boyks ran towards him saying: "What have you done? What have you done?" Botham says that he ran straight past Boycott and shouted: "I've run you out, you cunt!" I don't know if that's the truth, but it's Both's version.'

Boycott was devastated. Being out is a little death to any batsman, but to Boycott it feels like a mortal blow every time. He returned to the dressing-room saying: 'What am I doing, playing with children? What am I doing?' He covered his face with a towel and remained beneath it, mortified to his soul. Edmonds approached him – no one else would dare – and said: 'OK, Boyks, what are we doing now?' The despairing Boycott answered from beneath his towel: 'You and Willis are in charge of this tour – you work it out.' So England crashed the ball around for the rest of the evening, declared overnight at 96 for 4 and bowled New Zealand out next day. Boycott had captained England to victory.

Edmonds added: 'I get on tremendously well with Boyks. I remember talking to him after a county match when he'd been batting really slowly, asking him: how can you play like that? What kind of game are you playing? And he said: "Aye, but if you'd got me out, you'd have run through the lesser players." There was some truth in that, too.

'He can be aggravating to play with, but he's a top-liner. There's no doubt that in a Test match, when you've been slogging your guts out like Bob Willis, having bowled 20 or 30 overs, it must be awfully nice to see Boycott walking out to bat. You know you can take your boots off for a day and a half. Too often when you have finished bowling, you daren't even leave the ground. You can't go to the beach, you can't go to the hotel, and the nervous tension builds up again as you wait for the collapse to start again. But at the outset of an innings, Boyks is tremendous. Though it becomes a little tiresome to find him still patting back the half-volleys after 60 overs.'

Edmonds thoroughly enjoyed playing under Boycott's captaincy, despite his reservations about his excessively subjective approach: his desperate desire for a good personal performance as his main priority. But with Brearley, it was ever a different matter. Despite Brearley's unquestioned tactical grasp, for Edmonds, participation was always overshadowed by this gigantic collision of personalities. Naturally, it was a problem that expressed itself in cricketing terms.

Brearley's batting used to drive Edmonds up the wall. When Brearley was accepted as the great leader, his batting was treated with generosity by the critics, but in his earlier days as England captain, he received some wounding attacks on his playing abilities. Indeed, it was something of a triumph for Brearley to get picked as one of the troops, before his reputation for captaincy made him a giant.

Edmonds said: 'In the mid-seventies, Brearley moved himself up to open the batting. The old stager, Eric Russell, had disappeared from sight. Brears might have had his eye on an England place as he made this move, but given the type of player he is – "pawky" to use his own word – it made good sense. He needs a lot of overs to establish himself, a lot of overs to get any runs. This was fine when he was batting alongside Mike Smith, who was always a free scorer. But I'm sure that one of the things that caused problems between me and Brearley was that when Brears came in after scoring 60 runs in 70 overs, he would then tell me to go and have a slog for the team benefit. I should have said: "OK, Brears, you're the man in charge." But what I actually said was: "Well, fuck me, is this a team game, or what?" Probably this was the start of open conflict. I can remember many episodes like that. Certainly all the other players would be thinking it. But I was the only one saying it.' Of course.

'Yet I found it so easy to play cricket with Boyks. He would stand at mid-off and take the piss out of me when I was bowling. I knew he thought I was a good player, and that always helps. He might have been a terrible captain, but I found it easy to play under him. I could call him all kinds of names, ask him how could he play like that, patting back the half-volleys? He never took it the wrong way, was always prepared to argue his own position logically. He never took offence with me. But Brears – I could never talk with him. The constructive exchange of ideas was nil.'

Brearley was not too impressed with Edmonds' batting, come to that: a style 'which in antagonistic moods I would describe as a mindless combination of blocking and slogging'. There is a something about this description that has the ring of Edmonds about it. Edmonds concedes that he used to bat in a stupidly perverse way after Brearley's batting had driven him mad with frustration. Brearley's batting often exasperated Edmonds. Edmonds batting often had the same effect on his captain. 'You would be playing for a draw,' Brearley said, 'and they would have a defensive field, with one man in the deep. And Edmonds would invariably manage to put the ball down long leg's throat.'

But what, in the long run, annoyed Edmonds even more than Brearley's batting, was Brearley's failure to see Edmonds as a great bowler. Chanel No 5: Ian Gould's jibe crystallised in Edmonds' mind his own position in Brearley's scheme of things.

It was, Brearley insists, a cricketing judgement. He can offer a number of reasons as to why it was essential to have Edmonds operating as fifth choice bowler. Edmonds feels on his part that Brearley's judgement could not help but be affected by the growing friction between the two, the increasing irritation either man found with the other. Brearley could certainly find plenty of personal reasons for keeping Edmonds out of the attack. When Edmonds did come on there was always a confrontation between bowler and captain about the field placings. 'He has accused me both of wanting to over-attack and under-attack,' Brearley said. Edmonds, on his part, swears he never felt Brearley wanted to over-attack. The rows were generally over Edmonds' taste for an in-out field: a cluster round the bat and a man or two out at long-on/long-off to stop, perhaps catch, the big hit. Brearley's preference was for mid-on/mid-off to stop the pushed single, the aim being to pressure the batsman by drying up the flow of runs. But Edmonds wanted to leave the push shot as an option for the batsman, and thereby gain wickets: it was an impasse.

Brearley writes: 'Emburey and I always respected each other's ideas: if we differed I would generally let him try his way first, suggesting that he give mine a go if he was not successful. With Edmonds, however, there was rarely this productive willingness to differ. I think we both felt that the other failed to appreciate our point of view. What I interpreted as contempt for my ideas, he experienced as uncertainty about his ability to put it into effect. He thought I was unwilling to give him a long-off because I saw the opposition too much in my own pawky mould, while I felt he expected opposition batsmen to play in his style – which in antagonistic moods I would characterise as a mindless combination of blocking and slogging.'

Note here Brearley's measured tread from logical argument to straightforward abuse. It betrays the fact that the Edmonds situation got to him, and still rankles. Edmonds is genuinely furious about that little paragraph: he has never, he says, felt inhibited by any captain's desire to attack. He disagreed profoundly with Brearley's notion that the lack of a mid-off released pressure on the batsman. 'I want the batsman to push for one: I will have a short extra cover there for the catch when the push goes wrong. Or if the ball is turning, the attempted push will often give a catch at slip. Brears would never understand this – and I would go berserk.

'He talks about this constructive exchange of ideas with Embers: if it doesn't work out your way we'll try mine. Why didn't he say that to me? I always had to do it his way first.' Brearley, of course, says he often tried Edmonds' way, and so we are on our way into an oh-yes-I-did-oh-no-you-didn't situation. Cricketing disagreement, eh? The truth of the matter is that captain and bowler drove each other clean round the bend, and found it impossible to work together. The captain also happened to be captain of England. It is not utterly surprising, then, that Edmonds was not a regular in the England side. He was excluded on cricketing grounds – naturally!

Though one cannot expect Edmonds to be totally impartial when discussing Brearley – any more than we can expect Brearley to be the same about Edmonds – it is fascinating talking to Edmonds about Brearley's captaincy, and hearing some of his reservations about the man who carries this reputation for unadulterated excellence at the art. Brearley is traditionally believed to be the finest manipulator of the fragile egos of bowlers, and certainly the two most successful bowlers in English history, Botham and Willis, will go along with that assessment.

But if he brought the best from some, he inhibited other more humble bowlers. 'Brearley was a batsman-captain, and he gave the impression that he believed no bowler should ever bowl a bad ball,' Edmonds said. 'If you bowled a bad ball, he would kick the earth in frustration, as if his entire master-plan had gone awry. He put a lot of pressure on his bowlers in that way – Dermott Monteith, Simon Hughes, Embers in the early days, Mike Selvey. They'd be walking back to their mark thinking: "Oh no, the whole plan's gone wrong – and it's my fault!" It would upset some bowlers. It would annoy me, and I'd get distracted from bowling sometimes. Yet when he was talking about the opposition, it was as if he never received a bad ball in his life.' (Indeed, from watching him bat one might think that was almost literally the case.) 'Yet you had guys like Hughes so worried about ruining the plan by bowling a bad ball that he couldn't concentrate, and he would bowl worse, and Brearley just couldn't conceal his frustration.'

This story might have a slightly familiar ring to it. It was for this very reason – destroying other players' confidence by expressing annoyance – that Edmonds was sacked from the captaincy of his school. 'Absolutely right,' Edmonds conceded. 'If I was captaining now – 17 years later – I'd try not to fall into the same trap. Brears certainly showed the same flaw in his captaincy. Batsmen felt it too. Wilf Slack, fine player, was inhibited for years by his fear of making an error with Brearley at the other end.'

Edmonds has a considerable respect for the fact that Brearley was an exceptional captain and for the toughness in Brearley that made his captaincy possible. But he has no time at all for the Brearley myth. Brearley's reputation as the Solomon of captaincy followed the wonderful 1981 Ashes summer, in which Brearley took over the captaincy from Botham and reversed the flow of the series. Botham found himself again: ergo, Brearley made Botham. And yet, in two of those matches, England were in a losing position. At Headingley it took Botham's inspired slog, and at Edgbaston England were rescued from defeat, and handed victory, by Botham's five-wicket burst. Wisden said: 'for the second successive test, England contrived to win after appearing badly beaten.' 'What is the truth?' Edmonds asks. 'Did Brearley make Botham? Or did Botham make Brearley — and start the Brearley myth?'

Edmonds has never seen Brearley in mythical terms. Yet it was probably an error of judgement on Edmonds' part when he offered to punch the teeth of the England captain down his throat. Especially as it was in the middle of a Test match.

It happened at Perth in the 1978–79 series, when Brearley was leading a Packer-weakened English side against a Packer-ruined Australian team. It was a strange tour, conducted in an atmosphere of great bitterness and rancour, with Packer's World Series circus going on at the same time. The Australians took an immense dislike to Brearley, and his habit of beating the Australians and explaining why in a posh voice. He became the most hated English captain since Douglas Jardine. He was seen as the quintessence of all that is rotten in England: soft, prissy, devious, decadent, too clever by half, a show-off intellectual, and, in short, a poofter. Brearley once grew a beard, 'to roughen my exterior for contacts with the rebarbative Australians', as he said with characteristic earthiness. It didn't stop the Australians from shouting 'poofter' at him all the time, which he found understandably trying.

Edmonds was in the touring party (Underwood was with Packer) and played in the first Test, bowling a total of 13 overs without a wicket. He was included in the 12 for the second Test at Perth, but in the end had to carry the drinks. Bob Taylor kept wicket (Knott too was with Packer) and, loyal as ever to Captain Brears, said: 'Phil had been made twelfth man, and his attitude towards his duties was, to say the least, somewhat cavalier. We came off after one particularly tense session to find Phil with his feet up having done nothing about drinks. Mike (Brearley) tore a strip off him, and I'm sure some of the crowd outside heard the ructions. It was all water off a duck's back to Phil . . .' It is a typical Edmonds story, and as such, not true. Taylor is wrong on several counts, as both Brearley and Edmonds will tell you.

Edmonds had, in fact, got all the drinks and lunches ready and waiting for the players as they came off. Having set them all up, he fell into conversation with some spectators, and when the England team came off, he was the picture of a man with a 'sod the lot of you' attitude. But he had done his job adequately. Brearley was, as he led the team off, called a poofter again, Edmonds thinks. He went into the pavilion and slammed the door, and then thundered out again to order Edmonds back into the pavilion to look after the team. Edmonds said: 'I went into the pavilion, slightly perplexed, and I made the mistake of following Brears with my eyes as he was stalking around the room. And he started shouting at me again, telling me it was my job to look after the guys, and that he didn't want a drink, but if he did want one I should be there to bring it to him. This went on for five minutes.'

Brearley was already at boiling point, and Edmonds' blood was slowly creeping up to the 100 degree mark. At length, with the memory of seasons of frustration behind him, Edmonds burst from cover. He lost his temper as well, and then, chest to chest with the England captain, uttered the following unforgettable words: 'Get off my fucking back, Brearley, or I'll fucking fix you.'

He meant it. Brearley, too, was beside himself with anger. John Lever, an earthy Essex lad, intervened before these two Cambridge graduates could start thumping each other. 'I was very close to it,' Edmonds has acknowledged. 'I really wanted to stick one on him.'

'It was a mistake not be seen to be doing the job properly,' Edmonds said. Brearley said: 'It was, I think, more my fault than I have acknowledged. Phil had done all the things he should have done, I was hot, and I was tired, and I flew off the handle. He was sitting with his feet up, and I felt that there should have been more response from him. He would have said that to show more respect would have been crawling, no doubt. It was as if he really resented being twelfth man. But it is difficult in these circumstances to say if that was right, or how much my response was conditioned by my experience of him.

'He flew off the handle in response to the fact that I, unreasonably, flew off the handle. It was a real face-to-face. But I don't think I would have hit him. I have not hit anyone since I was a child.'

Brearley says that Edmonds, wrongly, saw this incident as a watershed in their relationship. Edmonds said: 'I didn't think much of it at the time. I thought it would just blow over.' Frances added: 'After all, it's just the sort of exchange of views Phil and I have every night.'

So then at tea-time, Edmonds was ready at the door to greet

the players back from the middle. 'Oh Brears,' he asked sweetly. 'Would you like a drink?' 'I was trying to break the ice, and at the same time make a point, but this was taken as insolence. Boyks came to me at the end of the day and said: 'You'd better get your swimming trunks out. Because you won't be playing any more cricket on this tour.' I laughed, and said I couldn't believe it. It was a row, but I thought it would pass over. I had been brought up at school to fight it out and forget it, in those boxing matches in the quad. I thought Brearley would forget that row in the same way.' But Edmonds did not play another Test match on the tour. Once again, he missed the chance to bowl on a real turner, on which Emburey and Geoff Miller bowled England to victory. And inevitably, this was followed by a match on an even better wicket – better if you happen to be a spin bowler – and Miller again profited, ending up with 23 Test wickets and the reputation of being a top-liner.

Brearley insists that the row did not affect his judgement and that Edmonds was left out on purely cricketing grounds. Certainly Brearley won the series, and that, in a sense, is the end of the argument. But it is worth remembering that Clausewitz, the German general of the Napoleonic era who wrote the definitive book of strategy, *On War*, once said, 'a purely military judgement is a distinction that cannot be allowed'. Brearley – unquestionably the Clausewitz of cricket – might well say the same thing of purely cricketing judgements.

Edmonds' international cricketing career did not, in fact, reach a dead halt in the Perth pavilion. Only his touring career. In the following domestic season, he was an England man again, and played under Brearley in the 1979 World Cup – the one in which England were beaten finalists. He played in England's opening game against Australia and, in his own shy, modest assessment, 'bowled well, fielded brilliantly'. But he also hurt his back, and later went into spasm and needed to be helped from the ground at close of play, and shoe-horned into the back of the Rancho, which Frances drove home.

He recovered in time to help England beat Pakistan in the third match, missed the semi-final when England beat New Zealand, and would have missed the final, too, but Willis broke down, and Edmonds was back in his place. It was a memorable match – and it was one of those days when Brearley's captaincy was not at its best.

'After the semi-final, I drove back from Old Trafford with Brearley. It was a bit of a tense trip. He kept saying: How can we possibly beat the West Indians? I felt then that he was not expecting to win, and that he was going to be satisfied with a good personal performance. I thought that then. It was rather cynical of me to think that.'

The West Indians batted first, and Edmonds bowled well. With 2 for 40, he was, albeit narrowly, the most effective bowler. 'I'll never forget, though, that after I had bowled about five overs, and bowled really well, he took me off and put Wayne Larkins on. There had never been any discussion of the possibility of Wayne bowling. And he went for 21 in two overs. Unbelievable. Well, in the same way that Both's better bowling performances will help him when he comes to bat, so the same thing happened in reverse with Wayne. He felt guilty at conceding all those runs. And he got nought.'

The West Indians made 286 in their 60 overs, with Viv Richards scoring 138. With hindsight, the England side looks extraordinary. For a start, they had only four bowlers, which meant that 12 overs had to be found from Boycott, Gooch and, as it transpired, Larkins. These three returned joint figures of 0 for 86. And then England opened their reply with Boycott and Brearley – neither of them Speedy Gonzales. They both played with immense caution, and fell wildly behind the clock. 'I'll never forget the scene in the dressing-room at tea,' Edmonds said. 'All the guys round the trolley were congratulating them, and Derek Randall was saying things like "Magic, skip. If one of you is there at the end, we've won it." And I was at the other end of the dressing-room, saying what is going on? We have to go and slog the weak links!'

At tea, England were 0 for 79 off 25 overs. Brearley looks back at this in his book and admits that at that point it was the time to cut loose. But in the next 13 overs, only 50 runs were added. The weak link in the West Indies attack, the overs Collis King and Richards had to find between them, were allowed to pass virtually unmolested. From 129 for 0, England plummeted to 192 all out as the need for slogging became desperate, the run rate required became more and more impossible, and Joel Garner bowled like a dream. Brearley admits that he was swayed into this false tactic of steady-as-she-goes by the comforting weight of dressing-room approval, and cites this as a dreadful warning to all captains: don't believe in the approval of your team-mates all the time. Well, he got no approval from Edmonds at any time in that match.

Frances remembers a further drive in the Rancho, when both were going to a Middlesex match shortly after the final. Edmonds was still burning with fury that the final had been flung away in so abject, so wimpish a fashion. Frances was also there: 'Phil kept feeding me apples so I wouldn't say anything out of turn, and Phil was so tense he nearly crashed the car on the motorway.'

There were not many good times left in the relationship. Admittedly, the following season, Edmonds became Middlesex vice-captain, but it was an unhappy business for them both. In fact, Edmonds said, in an interview he gave me for *The Times* in 1984, that 'Brearley manipulated for two years to get me out of the vice-captain's job.'

Brearley, on his part, says, knowing that Edmonds will not believe him, that it was not entirely down to him that Edmonds was not retained as vice-captain and the natural successor to Brearley. He says that he had been keen for Edmonds to have a go as vice-captain, and that in the end the message came over loud and clear from the rest of the team that they didn't want him to continue. That made the decision clear, especially as the policy at that time was to try out a number of people in the job. 'Brearley studiously refers to the decision-makers as we – and then revealingly slips up every now and then: 'We wanted to try others as well as Edmonds, and Gatting and Emburey were the other main contenders I had – I mean, we had in mind.'

Brearley says, with some accuracy, that Edmonds would have done better at a county with a weaker bowling attack, a side in which it was essential for him to bowl lots and lots of overs. Edmonds has his precariously low threshold of boredom, which affects him when he is waiting to bowl, and which fuels his impatience with life and captains. He said that Edmonds' notion of a good captain is one who lets him bowl a lot – which is true of all bowlers' relationships with all captains. And at Middlesex, Edmonds remained Chanel No 5.

No matter how many good cricketing reasons you can find for

Edmonds being left out here, dropped there and underbowled the other place, the fact remains that the problem was not in the cricket but in the people. Edmonds is, indeed, a maddening cricketer, but some captains have made that work for them. Edmonds can also be a maddening man. His reputation for awkwardness goes back some years. At one stage he was nicknamed 'Maggie' – because he was always leader of the opposition. That rather dates that particular reputation. Brearley said: 'You can take a certain amount, but you get fed up with people continually being flip and oppositional.'

Edmonds' reply to that would be that you can get equally fed up with people being nit-picking and schoolmasterly.

There is no doubt that Brearley has overshadowed Edmonds' cricket career, but there is a real sense in which Edmonds feels Brearley single-handedly wrecked it, merely by existing and being Brearleyesque. Their opposition was inevitable: it was unfortunate, then, for Edmonds to get so far on the wrong side of the most influential man in English cricket.

Edmonds traces many people's instinctive mistrust of him to the Brearley legacy. There is no denying that there is truth in that, but Brearley says: 'He has taken this belief to extremes. He has a view of people as being extremely calculating and manipulative, and I don't think that is true of me. The idea that I got in the way of his advancement after my retirement is nonsense.'

Yet it is true that English cricket's instinctive reactions of 'any one but Edmonds', or of 'this really is Edmonds' last chance', carried on for some seasons after Brearley's final retirement as England captain in 1981. Edmonds also continued to blow his chances through spurts of recklessness, or through errors of tact and diplomacy. 'I should have been nice to Brearley. I should have bitten everything back and said "of course, Brears, certainly Brears",' Edmonds said. 'If I'd been able to do that, I'd be captain of Middlesex now, and probably captain of England as well. But no, I always spoke out – I'm always incredibly stupid and naïve.'

When I met Brearley, I spoke of Edmonds' consistent failure to be diplomatic. Brearley's hot reaction to this took me aback: 'When people talk about being diplomatic, I often think that they believe they should be insincere in order to get by. I don't think that. Willis was not insincere, nor was he a great diplomat. No more was Botham or Gooch or Hendrick or Lever or Boycott. If Phil thinks you have to be a crawler to get on with me, he is wrong. You are bound to have strong characters in an England dressing-room. There have always been lively discussions and quarrels: teams are not always idyllically happy. A good team is full of conflict. To say that Edmonds should have been more diplomatic is a loaded way of putting it.'

My own view is that Edmonds should have left Middlesex a long time ago, and accepted one of the many tentative offers of captaincy from other counties. He would then have been able to bowl himself to death had he wanted, he could have tried being a master of tactics, and would generally have been cock of his own walk. Had he done so, he would have been considered for the England captaincy. And best of all, he would have got out from Brearley's shadow: that was the only way in which Edmonds could ever have 'fixed' Brearley. The Edmonds–Brearley conjunction was one that did no good to either man.

But there has always been a lot to keep him at Lord's. Firstly there is London, and business, 'and London is business', Edmonds believes. Edmonds is not the sort to be happy doing deals in provincial Rotary Clubs. He also likes Lord's: the tradition and the grandeur. He likes living in Kensington/Notting Hill, and he likes meeting City men for lunch – which you can't do from Leicester, or Southampton.

Then there is the 'benefit rut'. When your benefit year approaches, even if you loathe your captain, you don't feel like saying 'never mind the chance of making a hundred grand, I'm looking for cricketing fulfilment'. Then you have your benefit, and you feel that it is not the gentlemanly thing to do, to leave straight afterwards. In short, you get stuck.

And then there was the question of Brearley's retirement. Year after year, Edmonds believed Brearley was in his last season, and that the following summer he would be involved in his psycho-therapeutic pursuits. Year after year, Brearley stayed on for just one more season, addicted to cricket and winning and captaincy. Edmonds misread the situation, in fact.

And so Brearley really has been the dominant influence on Edmonds' cricket career, and thus on the greater part of his life. Why should it be so, why should two people form so intimate, and so destructive a relationship: one which started in liking and in a shared desire, of all the innocent things, merely to win cricket matches together? I cannot say.

Since his retirement, Brearley has written a number of pieces in *The Sunday Times*, for which he writes regularly, saying that Edmonds should be selected for this match, or that tour. In his book, he is at pains to say some nice things about Edmonds, as well as various less nice things. He rejects any suggestion from Edmonds that this might be a technique by which he is, like a doctor, burying his mistakes. He says that most of their disagreements, and all the reasons for Edmonds' exclusions, were cricketing ones.

In his turn, Edmonds has said some scathing things about England teams from his own pulpit in the media. His most memorable phrase has been his description of selectoral policy as a pursuit of 'malleable mediocrity'. It goes back to Edmonds' feelings about the English love of the half-baked.

But Edmonds said: 'When Brears and I meet these days, we are good mates again. The tensions from the cricket field have gone.'

Brearley said: 'I confess that I am upset that he feels my retirement was his biggest break in cricket. I find it hurtful. I have regrets about the way things turned out between us. I have had other difficult players to captain before, but it worked less well with him than with anyone. I am glad he has found his success now. I honestly hope it will continue.'

Edmonds said: 'There are so many things I admire, and like, about Brears. In purely cricketing terms, he is the best captain I have ever seen. The tremendous thing was the way in which we were always trying to achieve something positive in the field when Brears was in charge. Even when the situation warranted a defensive action, it was positive defence, with a constructive aim in mind. We were not meandering about aimlessly, as has happened with some England captains.

'Also, Brears is probably the hardest man you will ever meet. Mentally, he is extraordinarily tough. I remember an occasion at Old Trafford, at the semi-final of one of the one-day competitions, at a time when Brears was having a lean spell with the bat for England. We were in the field, and Brears was having a nightmare, with the ball following him around, and he fumbling it at every opportunity, much to the delight of the Lancashire crowd. Brears took some frightful abuse. But he made a point of placing himself in the most important fielding position of the moment, at short mid-wicket to a leg-side player. Lesser men would have found somewhere to hide.

'Similarly, on the 1979–80 tour of Australia, there was a lot of controversy about fielding circles in one-day matches. The macho Aussies and, naturally, the media were running riot, insisting that the Pommie poofters played with circles. But in the middle of it all, Brears was saying quietly: 'I'm sure that these circles are a very good idea, but we have never played with them before and would find it hard to adjust all at once.' Not only were the matches played without circles, but in one of them, Brears put the wicket-keeper on the boundary when they needed four off the last ball to win – despite the terrible abuse he knew he would get.

'But his toughness, his ruthlessness, are concealed by the old velvet glove: his quiet, inoffensive, articulate demeanour – another admirable quality. I think, though, that despite this toughness, Brears, possibly because of his interest in psychotherapy, became excessively sensitive, in a rather narcissistic way. Take the big black beard he grew for the tour in Australia, for example.

'I sometimes wonder if our personality clash could have been avoided, or whether it was the inevitable result of human chemistry. It was unfortunate that our relationship soured to such an extent that all I could see in a man of indubitably excellent qualities were his little mincing steps and his bitchiness towards me.' Hell hath no fury . . .

For the most part, Brearley's attempts to work his arts of captaincy on Edmonds were a failure. Brearley may have a degree in people, but there was one course in which the professor of captaincy flunked out: the course on the life and works of Philippe Henri Edmonds.

> Nice, nice, very nice,
> Nice, nice, very nice,
> Nice, nice, very nice,
> So many different people
> In the same device.

CHAPTER 7

THE GOOD TOURIST

The worst thing that can happen to any cricketer is to share a room with Edmonds. For a start, the man only sleeps four hours a night. Also, he loathes having the curtains closed. The best you can do is to strike a deal with him, as Tim Robinson did in India, and have the curtains closed every other night. 'It strikes me as totally stupid to blindfold yourself to go to sleep,' Edmonds said. 'Doubtless this is because of my Zambian upbringing, and sleeping under the stars.' Edmonds cuts into his room-mates' day from both ends: he doesn't sleep till late, and he wakes early. He needs the light on, preferably all through the night, because he is always reading. He reads continually and obsessively. His mind is seething and restless and he thinks sleep is a waste of time. His bed is constantly covered in newspapers: in England he gets the complete range of national papers, including the *Financial Times* but excluding *The Sporting Life*. Abroad, he gets airmail editions of the English press, and any other English language papers and news magazines available. This brew will be seasoned with sheaves of company reports and balance sheets, property prospectuses and his business correspondence. He will also have half a dozen books on the go at any one time, and again, the breadth of his interest is considerable: histories, biographies, political diaries, great novels, thrillers. He read Kipling in India, and a book alleging a global plot to assassinate Pope John-Paul I called *In God's Name*, which was an intoxication to a man for whom the conspiracy theory is the first donné in any political discussion.

All this would be bad enough for his roomie, but there is worse. While Edmonds is sitting up through the night, or in the early morning, he doesn't just read. He also listens to the radio. The BBC World Service shall follow him wherever he goes. He listened to the World Service when he was a boy in Zambia, and he listens to it at home in Kensington. He listens to it everywhere he goes on tour, comparing with utter absorbtion the BBC reports on the unrest that followed the assassination of Indira Gandhi with the reports in *The Times of India*. To a man with the conspiracy theory in mind, it was a fascinating period.

Edmonds is a complete World Service junkie, addicted to both the flow of information and the background murmur of voices. He also listens to Radio Moscow and the Voice of America, and revels in 'comparing their propaganda'. To room with Edmonds is to wake up to *Farming Today*, and that after you have already been woken at three in the morning by *Just a Minute*, or *The British Press Review*. 'There was almost a divorce when I woke up in the middle of the night to hear him listening to a recipe for toffee apples,' said Frances. 'Gourmet toffee apples,' Edmonds said. 'You should make some for me.'

Paul Downton has roomed with Edmonds and reports that Edmonds was very considerate. He has no memories of *Gardeners' Question Time* muttering into his dreams. Downton happens to be a very heavy sleeper. When Edmonds shared with Jonathan Agnew in India in 1984–85, the two established a routine. Last thing at night (last thing by Agnew's standards, anyway) they ordered a cup of tea and a cup of cocoa. The cocoa came in a little pot that was covered in a sort of cocoa cosy. If you were extremely careful, you could slip the cosy over the light bulb at an angle, so that the light fell on Edmonds' books but left poor old Agnew in semi-darkness.

Graeme Fowler had one of those dark nights of the soul in India on the same tour after he had gone down with the disease that affects so many visitors to the subcontinent – the sort of disease that is a great help if you need to work at your speed between the wickets. Throughout the night, virtually every hour, Fowler would spring awake with horror in his eyes and sprint for the sanctuary of the bathroom. He would then return from his ordeal – and every time there was Edmonds, still awake, placidly reading the same book, the radio chattering beside him, on and on until daybreak.

Morning came to find Fowler utterly exhausted, and Edmonds, with a spring in his step, listening to *Yesterday in Parliament* before breakfast.

Edmonds loves touring. As his mad reading habits demonstrate, he has an unending curiosity about the world and how it works. 'Sportsmen who represent their country are in a privileged position,' he said. 'We go round the world doing something we enjoy, and get treated like kings while we do it. We stay in the best hotels, someone else looks after travel problems, baggage and customs. This is particularly evident in India, where top cricketers are virtually deified. Our privileges stand out starkly against the general chaos and confusion of the place. We are so pampered it is easy to get totally blasé. It was a shock, going from India to Australia and being expected to carry our own bags.

'Another tremendous privilege of playing cricket at top level is the people you can meet, if you want to. International sport, and particularly cricket, in Commonwealth countries attracts the elite from all walks of life: politicians, businessmen, scientists and entertainers. This is particularly true on tour, with all the official functions, High Commissioners' cocktail parties and so on. Most of the guys find these a real bore, and talk about 'ear-bashing'. I enjoy them. How else could one meet such a concentration of the country's elite in such a short time?'

Most professional cricketers like Australia best and Pakistan least: Ian Botham, the Oscar Wilde of English cricket, summed up the cricketers' feelings about Pakistan when he said that it was the ideal place to send your mother-in-law for a holiday. But Edmonds was fascinated by Pakistan.

'I toured Pakistan in 1977–78 – a very interesting time in the country's history,' Edmonds said. 'The premier, Bhutto, had just been deposed by the army, and General Zia had taken over, and was chief law administrator. Inevitably, there were political tensions – exacerbated by the fact that Bhutto was in jail. To an outsider, it seemed that life would have been simpler for the new régime had Bhutto been killed in the coup. Instead, he was embarrassingly alive, and a figurehead for any subversive activities.

'And so it was inevitable that cricket became a focal point for political activity. Martial law had been imposed, and that meant that if more than four people gathered together, they were considered to be a riot – unless they were at a cricket match. The Bhutto faction, led by Mrs Bhutto, naturally took advantage of this to initiate mass meetings at the cricket, and so there were real riots on successive days of the Lahore Test match. Mind you, the riots themselves said a lot about the way the country worked. Once the rioters had stopped the cricket and made their point, they then cleared up the mess they had made and demanded that the cricket should continue. Very logical, I thought!

'General Zia himself turned out to be a fascinating personality. Many of the High Commission people and industrialists I met felt that he was a compromise choice from the army elite – and who would be quickly replaced, once things had settled down. But these people – and probably most of the Western world with them – underestimated the growth of Muslim fundamentalism, which General Zia supports solidly. It was a strange time to visit a country. I noticed that in Rawlpindi, the cricket attracted smaller crowds than the public floggings the next day.

'To be a cricketer touring places like India and Pakistan teaches you an enormous amount about the British legacy to these places – and the influence of the BBC World Service. I met the headmaster of an independent British run college in Peshawar, Edward's College, it was called. Virtually every general's son and every cabinet minister's son had been educated there: and afterwards at university or technical college or military academy in Great Britain. Think how much influence Britain had in the country, then.

'But the government was, at that time, just about to cancel the minute subsidy they gave that kept the school running. So I've no doubt now that the general's sons now further their education in America, or the Soviet Union, or Peking. But visiting these countries, and meeting the top men, gives you a special interest in the affairs of the country and the careers of its leaders.'

This immensely positive attitude to touring has not prevented Edmonds from winning the reputation of being a bad tourist. He has been left out of more touring parties than he has had hot curries. The selectors have always managed to find some good cricketing reason to leave him out – for example, they found it essential to take three off-spinners to Australia in 1982–83 – but the real reason has been a great reluctance to put up with the imagined horrors of his presence for three months and more. Such a prospect strikes terror

1 This picture is included as a matter of historical interest. It shows Edmonds with hair, at his most appealing, and at the height of his 'blond Adonis' period.

2 Majid Khan of Pakistan – and Cambridge.

3 'The slower you bowl, the more aggressive you must be,' says Edmonds. That must be why he pulls such extraordinary faces when he lets go of the ball.

4 (Right) Mike Brearley: the guru of cricket and the Bhagwan of captaincy. Edmonds does not see him in quite this light, however. Brearley here attired as an honoured guest at the England team's Christmas fancy dress party in India, 1981.

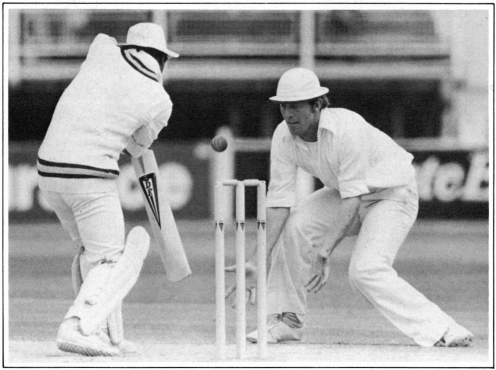

5 (Top) 'Will you build me one like that when *I* die?'

6 (Bottom) How to make friends and influence people.

7 The great all-rounder puts the attack to the sword. Edmonds, believe it or not, has three first class centuries to his credit. Here, he is on the way to scoring 48 for England against India at Bombay in 1984.

8 Counting popularity. He has just taken a ridiculously good catch to dismiss Boyd-Moss in the 1984 NatWest semi-final at Lord's.

9 Edmonds fielding in his favourite position. His low threshold of boredom has had a crucial bearing on his entire cricket career.

10 That's what it's all about: the most perfect slow bowling action in cricket.

11 A fine study of Edmonds puffing out his cheeks and wearing a silly hat. Both are much cherished characteristics: as are effort, eccentricity and aggression.

12 (Inset) Go on punk, make my day. Edmonds doing his Clint Eastwood bit against India. 'I find it easy to switch on the competitive spirit,' he said.

into the hearts of selectors among whom, inevitably, the captain always has the loudest voice. No one could imagine Edmonds 'Mucking In'.

For one of the most cherished values of an England touring side is the ability to Muck In. Social committees, japes, fancy dress parties and silly fines are all part of a touring side's life: in the 1984–85 tour to India, Gatting was fined for being fat. A lot of the mucking-in ethic operates on the same intellectual level. 'It is easy to get the reputation for being a sourpuss,' Edmonds said. Frances said: 'It is difficult to grasp the nuances of what it is exactly that constitutes a "good tourist". But on the basis of objective analysis, it would in some cases be someone who spends a lot of time propping up the bar and endeavouring, at all costs, to get the touring leg over. If you prefer ginseng tea to several pints a night, you are failing to be one of the lads, and if you have the cosmically subversive desire to do your own thing and be your own man, you are probably well on the way to being a bad tourist.' David Gower added that Edmonds was always an aloof figure, with his books and his Walkman. Nor is Edmonds likely to find the lads queueing up to swap cassettes: he got through the India tour with the copious assistance of Ludwig van Beethoven, deciding that all nine symphonies had an acceptable strength-for-weight ratio. Since the tour turned out to be Edmonds' personal Eroica, it would seem to have been a sound choice.

'Even at top level, the old amateur ideas of mucking in and making do persist,' Edmonds said. 'We go around the world, for months at a time, and at 35 years of age I am too old for the dormitory ethic. I like an occasional bit of privacy, so I am deemed not to be a team man. But in fact, I think now that it is more acceptable, to want to be an individual.' There is also the point that no one is surprised by Edmonds' behaviour any more. Eccentricity and aloofness are expected: that's Henri for you. Being part of the team – a successful part of a successful team in India – made Edmonds' desire for occasional bursts of solitude acceptable. But what helped the most is that the novelty value of Edmonds' peculiarities has worn off, in the same way that the shock of Botham's racketiness has faded away. Both men are now accepted – at the time of writing at least – as normal parts of an England party. Edmonds said: 'I think a number of cricketers have suffered from being seemed to be outsiders. Though Alan Knott was always treated well, considering that he never drinks, and is a bit of a hypochondriac. Well, that's Knotty, they said. It helped that he is such an inoffensive fellow, a genuinely nice guy who never throws his weight around, besides being a genius behind the stumps. I have never been enamoured of the schoolboy ethic of Mucking In – but I have always enjoyed touring tremendously.'

The schoolboy side of touring is always likely to be a problem for Edmonds. Even as a schoolboy, he didn't have much of a schoolboy side, and seemed a grown-up to his school-mates. As I have said, he always appears to be older than people of the same age. Dressing up and playing silly games is not really his cup of beer. When the Christmas fancy dress party came along in India, Allan Lamb dressed himself up from head to toe as an untouchable, Lamb being one of the greatest muckers-in and socialisers in the history of cricket, while Edmonds found the whole precedure slightly embarrassing. 'My self-conscious streak comes out, and I find it all such a load of nonsense, I really do. Left to my own devices, I would never say, "Come on guys, it's Christmas, let's all dress up!" But Lamby and Both and people love it. I don't know if they bow to pressure outside, the feeling that they should be doing something like that. I think that is the case with some people, a kind of enjoying yourself by numbers. It's Christmas, we've got to have a good time. The boys in Stalag 19 had a Christmas party too, didn't they? It's the same attitude.'

Edmonds went to the fancy dress party as a sheik, the principal points of the costume being dark glasses and a cheque book. This at least had a degree of appropriateness, Edmonds being as notorious for his financial manoeuvrings as any member of the Saudi royal house. (In fact Edmonds' room-mate of the time, Neil Foster, won the prize, for his disturbingly epicene performance as an Indian girl, beautifully made up and clad in a saree he had bought for his wife. 'He looked so natural in it,' said Edmonds wonderingly.)

Many people find travel, especially travel over long periods, a vexatious business. Touring is unquestionably wearing, and immensely stressful. Cricketers are incessantly battling an unnerving dual assault of pressure on the pitch and boredom round the hotel. But Edmonds loves being abroad, and has a curiosity about the world that goes a long way beyond cricket. Edmonds also relishes trips up-country, away from the five-star hotel belt. He remembers vividly a day in the Khyber Pass, when an influential person he had met took him to the smugglers' centre of Landikotal. But many of his colleagues loathe all this, and agree with Uncle Matthew in Nancy Mitford's *The Pursuit of Love*, that 'abroad is absolutely bloody and foreigners are fiends'. Australia just about passes muster, and so, say some, does South Africa, the principal delights being barbecues and beaches and beer. Western ladies are also available at both places. But many an Englishman cannot cope with the curries and culture-shock of the subcontinent.

Edmonds loves curries and culture-shock. 'Wherever I've been in the world, we've been looked after really well, and the food has always been adequate at the very least. Though I appreciate the efforts Bernard Thomas, the physio, made on the tour to India, to make sure the food was passable.' (Indeed, the only person to get spectacularly sick on that tour was Tony Brown, the manager. He fell out with a prawn cocktail, of all things. Perhaps Delhi, 700 miles from the sea, is not the best place in the world for shellfish.)

Tours to the subcontinent tend to be characterised by determined and rather xenophobic attempts to maintain the spirits of the more fragile souls by providing them with familiar food. 'When I went to Pakistan, it was incumbent on all the non-playing guys to make banana sandwiches for the rest. Waiters were coming in with these magnificent feasts of curries and fresh fruit, and I got the reputation for not being a good boy because I didn't make banana sandwiches. On that tour they also brought out a load of tins of Spam. So we had Spam sandwiches and banana sandwiches for lunch. And believe it or not, when we went to India in 1984, we took thousands of tins of corned beef – corned beef from Argentina. We'd just fought a war, and spent billions of pounds trying to beat these Argentinians, and then I walk into the headquarters of English civilisation, namely Lord's, and find box upon box of Argentinian corned beef.'

Not every cricketer has the resilient stomach and mind of Edmonds, however. Many get homesick, and the exaggerated team chumminess is an extension of this. But Edmonds never gets homesick. For a start he doesn't have a home to get sick for, not a home in the sense that most people understand the term. He has instead a pleasant living module in London. He and Frances have no children, and in the daily course of their lives, they thrive on separation, Edmonds off playing cricket around England and the world, Frances charging round Europe speaking half-a-dozen languages non-stop at top-level conferences. There is no cosy family circle for Edmonds to pine for.

The team spirit of a touring side regularly degenerates into something Bob Taylor called 'siege mentality'. Taylor, one of the great gents of our time, has freely admitted that there have been occasions when he has not walked when caught behind, as a direct result of the tourist's siege mentality – the feeling that 'all the foreigners are out to get us, we've got to stand back to back, lads, and we'll have to knock 'em out to get a draw'. Again, this is something that Edmonds is largely immune to. So much so that he finds tales of the Great Siege Mentality Tour of India in 1981–82 almost incomprehensible. Keith Fletcher was in charge. India won the opening Test, and thereafter the series degenerated into the most abysmal succession of footling draws that any one can remember. India slowed the over-rate down to absurd levels, and England's response was to slow them down even more. It was probably the most boring tour in living memory: all the journalists hated it, all the players loathed it. It was a tour characterised by a belief that the umpires were totally incompetent at the very least, and by a monstrous dog-in-the-manger approach to the cricket. Fletcher, the wily old county pro who was seen as a long-term successor to Brearley, was instantly replaced as captain – by Bob Willis, of all the unwily people. It was inevitable that this should happen after a series when the cricket was unacceptable throughout.

Edmonds – allegedly the gamesman's gamesman – cannot believe the lack of sportsmanship; the lack of mutual regard; the lack of fun that characterised Fletcher's tour. 'Of course there is always a lot of pressure on the Indians to win at home. Of course they weren't going to let us into the game. But to bowl at ten overs an hour – that was incredible. Why travel 5,000 miles to play such appalling cricket? I would say, forget about what they do, here's what we are going to do. I know it's easy to say now, and I know how some of the players there would have responded: if we bowl 15 overs an hour, it just gives them a chance to score runs quickly and so gives them more time to bowl us out twice. That may well be true. But it's just not in my nature to say, well you gave us 60 balls an hour to score, so we are going to give you 55. This may indicate a weak strain in my character – but I just don't think it matters that much whether you win or lose.

'I find it hard to reconcile my own feelings here. No matter how competitive I am on the field, and how hard I am trying to get guys out, I really do believe and always have believed that it is far more important to play a good game of cricket than to win. That might sound extremely naïve, coming from a so-called ultra-competitive individual. But many cricketers start to think like that as soon as they stop playing. The difference is that I am still playing. But you listen to guys like Willis or Robin Jackman doing their commentary stints, and they are saying how stupid the players are, how they should be throwing the bat and trying for a result, because it doesn't actually matter if they lose. And it doesn't!'

And indeed, that ineffably tedious Indian tour had one result that everyone has forgotten, and another result that is still talked about. Result one was the score: 1–0 to India. Result two was the rebel tour to South Africa. Edmonds is morally certain that a number of people went on that trip not just for the money, but because they were bored to the soul with Test cricket after that tour. And it was a tour, remember, that followed the wonders of the Ashes summer of 1981. A few months of tour brought morale from sky-high down to bootlace level.

The rebel tour was another trip Edmonds didn't go on. This time, however, he was asked. Or at least, approached. But it seems that once again the Edmonds reputation got in the way – though this time in a different fashion. John Emburey telephoned Edmonds from South Africa, asking him to join the tour. There was a frantic chase-round at the time for a couple of late additions to the squad. News had already got round that leading players were getting sums like £40,000 for the trip. Any professional cricketer would be interested in hearing more, of course, and Edmonds said he wanted to hear more about the finances before he committed himself. He told Emburey that it was all very well to say, 'jump on the next plane, you're playing on Tuesday'. How much money was involved?

'There is no way I would have gone to South Africa,' Edmonds said. 'But being inquisitive by nature, I wanted to get as much information as possible on the financial aspects of the tour.' Many cricketers got carried away at the thought of this lovely money machine out in South Africa. Edmonds was not one of them.

Emburey said he would call back, but never did: it seemed that the Edmonds reputation for wheeler-dealing had got in the way.

Many of the Breweries cricketers, in particular the captain Graham Gooch, could not believe that they were banned from Test cricket for three years, and still insist that this was a reasonable attitude to hold. They don't like to be told they were naïve. Edmonds, with rather more political acumen, predicted a long ban at the time, and was surprised that three years was all the players received. Edmonds saw the political implications of the tour at once. Before England had arrived in India, Mrs Gandhi had refused to allow Geoff Boycott and Geoff Cook into the country because of their South African connections. They were allowed in after they had each made statements about their abhorrence of apartheid. Mrs Gandhi was making a political point to her third world neighbours. When Boycott followed that statement by becoming a star name on the rebel trip, he and the rest of the side were making a fool of Indira Gandhi, a fool of the Test and County Cricket Board, and, by extension, the British government. 'Mrs Gandhi had scored points with the third world by showing reluctance to admit Cook and Boycott, and she had scored points at home by allowing the tour to go ahead after all. Now the cricketers were kicking sand in her face. Naturally there was going to be a long ban,' Edmonds said. The Edmonds appreciation of realpolitik was unerring.

That then, was the result of a bad tour. But touring is always a strain, always draining physically and spiritually. There are plenty of good bits – you read any tour diary ever published – but there are also the slow bits, when people get tired, homesick and fed up, and if performances and results are going the wrong way, the tour can disintegrate. The classic example of this happened with Allan Border's young Australian side in 1985 which, having been on the wrong end of a hiding, collapsed abjectly and suddenly, and wanly accepted a second. It was a distressing moral débâcle after they had played well for a long time – and it was right at the end of the tour that it happened. Touring cricketers get fed up with each other, the management, the country they are in, and with cricket. All of which happened to the England party at the end of the 1984–85 tour to India – when they went on a tourette of Australia to contest the so-called World Championship of Cricket, a spurious one-day tournament.

It was mostly day–night cricket, with white balls, coloured clothes, mascara under the eyes to minimise the floodlight glare, and lots of lolly and television. India won it, bursting with pleasure at getting away from the atmosphere of disapproval that followed their series defeat by England. England lost three out of three, which was a pretty poor show.

The trouble was that the party fell apart as soon as it arrived in Australia. The well-travelled members of the party had many friends in Australia, and they reacted to arriving in Australia after a tour of India like men in a desert coming upon a beer machine. They vanished in a trice, to beer, beaches and barbies, chased the women and drank the wine and had a high old time of it. The rest of the party got called 'the also-rans'.

The also-rans got lumbered with most of the official functions, and to make things worse, the management got cross with *them* when there was but a meagre party gathered to show the flag for the 'ear-bashings'. Naturally, the non-disappearing tourists were unhappy. This, combined with the relief every one naturally felt after three intense months in India, made the England part in the World Championship a complete anti-climax. The corporate will to win drowned somewhere off Bondi Beach. Edmonds, who can switch competitive instinct on and off at will (certainly he can switch it *on* any time he wants), was disappointed by the crumbling of corporate resolve that had been established in India, though he feels it was inevitable. Edmonds loves the big occasions, loves the night game, and finds the razzmatazz and the coloured clothing bring out his show-off, in-the-thick-of-the-action side rather than his self-conscious streak. He was desperately disappointed that things went so badly, and sees it as completely inevitable that it should happen after a long and difficult tour. The mistake was probably going.

Also, Edmonds, unlike many cricketers, finds Australia less than paradise. He is not a beer and barbie man. 'It's a nice place, but I'm not bowled over by beaches. The hotels are no better than the ones in Bombay. Australia is tremendous fun, but the sub-continent is much more interesting. I enjoyed being in India far more than being in Australia. I come from Africa which has, among the white population, the same kind of culture as Australia, outdoor, very sporty – and the funny thing is that I find Australia much more alien than Pakistan and India. In fact, the more I tour, the more I appreciate Europe. Not just England – I mean Europe: France and Italy, especially Tuscany and Rome.'

Frances added, gleefully quoting Edna Everage: 'The reason we Australians are so good at sport is the sun, the sand, the sea, the steaks, the outdoor existence and the total lack on any intellectual distraction.' Both of them feel that so many of the former colonies, especially the white-dominated ones, are, in their hearts, provincial. Whereas a European is a man of the world.

But there are intellectual distractions to be found throughout a cricket tour, if you are interested. Edmonds delights in the privilege of being an honoured guest in a country, and in that chance playing cricket gives one, of meeting all the leading people. He has a hunger for information, and like the elephant's child, an insatiable curiosity. That makes him an enthusiastic traveller. Your average cricketer prefers the bounding physical life of barbies and beers, but Edmonds would sooner meet General Zia. When Mike Gatting had to explain to the lads the political problems thrown up by the assassination of Percy Norris in India, he didn't really need to give Edmonds his lecture. 'I suffered it with wry amusement,' Edmonds said. 'Gatt is a tremendous fellow, but he wouldn't know a political nicety if he found one in a cheese and pickle sandwich.'

Yet Edmonds remains famous not as a tourist, but as a man who missed virtually every tour going. At the end of 1985, he had been on just three, and he first played first-class cricket in 1972. It is an extraordinary record. He toured Pakistan and New Zealand in 1977–78, the tour on which Brearley broke his arm and Boycott took over the captaincy, a tour on which Edmonds did well. (He also telephoned home at Christmas and, Frances recalls, reported that 'we have a complete madman out here'. It was a man new to touring, whom Edmonds recalls driven crazy by the boredom of not being in the team. A chap called Ian Botham.) He went the following winter to Australia under Brearley, and played one Test, after which Edmonds and Brearley had their terrible row. And after that, he did not tour until 1984–85, when he was the lynch-pin of the attack, bowled 276 Test match overs and was joint leading wicket-taker.

On that tour he was both successful as a cricketer and accepted as a man who, despite his occasional Garboesque pleasure in solitude, was a good tourist. The two were not unrelated: when not playing, especially during the nightmare tour with Brearley, frustration and boredom has eaten into the Edmonds soul. Frances said: 'He is very difficult as a non-playing tourist, and after he had had the aggro with Brearley, he was quite insufferable. Some players take not playing fairly well. I suppose they look at alternatives and think, well, I'd rather be here than there.' But that philosophy does not commend itself to Edmonds in the slightest, any more than it helped Botham when he was a left-out sprog in Pakistan, running amok with the shaving foam. In fact, as a cricketer, Edmonds is like the actor who asked the director what he was supposed to do in the pauses. 'What pauses?' asked the director, who prided himself on his pacey productions. 'You know – the pauses when other people are speaking.'

But being an accepted part of the England set-up does not make Edmonds act all humble. Nothing has that effect on Edmonds. Before the 1985–86 tour to the West Indies, he put in a request for a single room, knowing that only captain and vice-captain are allowed a room to themselves. The idea of giving Edmonds a single room is something that all his former room-mates would vote for, however fond of Edmonds they might be. Edmonds feels that cricket is a big money game these days, and does not see why the cost of an extra room should not be found. The reasons for room-sharing are partly for economy and partly for forging of team solidarity. Indeed, many of the cricketers actually prefer the sharing arrangement as an antidote to homesickness. Few actually seek solitude. However, Edmonds' request for a single room was turned down, inevitably, perhaps. 'Why should people be inconvenienced because their living habits are incompatible?' Edmonds is always a trier, and indeed, he has a point.

The traditional attitudes to touring, however, amuse him more than anything else. 'You talk to some of the experienced pros, they will tell you that the third tour is the dangerous one. The first tour is new and exciting, and you are learning. I don't know what, but you're supposed to be learning all the time. I thought you were just playing cricket, but no, you're learning. The second is new to the extent that it is a different place, but by the end of it, you are beginning to wonder. And by the third, about halfway through, you think – shit! What am I doing here in this place for four months when I could be home with the wife and kids?'

What makes Edmonds remorseful is the sudden feeling, when playing this game miles from home, that he really ought to be doing something serious. If it wasn't for cricket he could be out there making a million. He is still un joker qui joue au cricket. And there are about a million things he wants to do and deals he wants to strike, but cannot because the demands of cricket – and the rediscovered demands of touring – take huge bites into his time.

And yet the lure of touring might yet see him postpone his retirement once again. He has been talking about retirement at the end of the 1986 season, but nagging away at the back of his mind is the knowledge that he failed to do himself justice on his last Test-playing tour of Australia and utterly failed to leave with any credit or kudos after that four-month nightmare under Brearley. There is a part of him that longs to do an Ashes tour properly ... and another part that would sooner see him with his elbows on a board-room table.

But as he prepared to leave for the West Indies tour, he was still saying how much fun touring has always been. Touring, he says, is a great pleasure. This was so much the case that his colleagues on the Indian trip could not understand how it was that he had been cast as the monster to end all cricketing monsters, the man that most captains would not dare take on tour. In the end, Edmonds was heavily fined – for the crime of not being a trouble-maker. The monster was not just a match-winner. He was a good tourist to boot. The expectations of a nation had been betrayed.

CHAPTER 8

HARD TIMES

Edmonds propounds the conspiracy theory of history with great glee and even greater frequency. Power, corruption, realpolitik, the devious and self-serving ends of all establishments – these are subjects that fascinate him. Cricketing colleagues are hardly surprised by these interests: they see Edmonds as an arch-Machiavellian: a man who has devoted his life to working out what is in it for him. When he captained Middlesex as Mike Brearley's stand-in, his leadership was always based, so his colleagues devoutly believed, on a policy of manoeuvring to bowl on a wearing wicket, the ultimate aim being not victory but wickets for Edmonds that would win him a place on the winter's tour of India. The truth of the allegation scarcely matters: what is relevant is that it was believed. It was inevitable that such a notion should be accepted: it has long been an accepted fact that Edmonds is the most devious man in cricket.

Edmonds always thinks twice before acting. Edmonds always has his eye on the main chance. Edmonds only ever acts for number one and whenever he does anything generous, you wonder about the policy that lies behind the niceness. Edmonds is a schemer: a cold, calculating schemer. Small wonder that he is mistrusted.

He reads the *Financial Times* in the dressing-room, which makes him a suspicious character for a start. There are about as many *FT* readers in cricket dressing-rooms as there are readers of *Pravda*, and they are regarded with equal suspicion. Edmonds loves cooking up deals: you can hear him doing so on the dressing-room payphone, talking in terms that might as well be in Chinese so far as most cricketers are concerned: share issue, business expansion schemes, take overs, commerical properties – this man is weird! Cricketers watch Edmonds' financial juggling like children watching conjuring tricks. But for all that, it is not Edmonds the intriguer that is the prime mover on the cricket field. There, the dominant characteristic is the complete opposite: a total recklessness.

It has been said that the most compelling aspect of live theatre is the sense of danger that the finest, strangest actors can conjure up. There is no telling what they might do. An enraptured audience believes they might run amok through the stalls, murdering as they go. Laurence Olivier can give the impression of a complete and terrifying recklessness; other great performers can fill the air with a whiff of madness. When the Edmonds blood runs hot, he too has this streak of unselfconscious wildness.

Tim Lamb (secretary of Middlesex County Cricket Club) has a favourite Edmonds story, and one which illustrates the Edmonds recklessness perfectly. 'It was breakfast-time at a typical seaside hotel somewhere, all heavy silver, old ladies and people reading the *Daily Telegraph*. The service was incredibly slow, and all the players were grumbling and muttering about getting a bacon sandwich on the way to the ground. But Phil stood up and started yelling at the top of his voice: "Help! Help me! I'm starving to death!"' Other versions of the story have Edmonds crawling about the room howling in agony and expiring on the carpet.

But it is Edmonds' alleged deviousness that inspires mistrust. Selectors have been reluctant to pick him for England because of fears of what he might get up to. County colleagues have seen his deviousness as a reason to remove him from the county captaincy. But in fact, it has always been his recklessness that has got him into trouble: that, and the fact that people's expectations are geared to unconventional behaviour from Edmonds.

Bob Taylor says that Edmonds seems to have a professional death-wish. There is something of truth in this. Edmonds is incapable of acting with care and circumspection, especially on a cricket field when competition heats the blood. (It is odd that he is criticised for deviousness. The most spectacular example of deviousness in the history of cricket involved players virtually all of whom were and still are regarded as good ol' pros: the 'rebels' who went on the secret South African Breweries trip in 1982. Graham Gooch writes about the deviousness involved in his book, *Out of the Wilderness*, and says, 'What else could we do?' What indeed?)

If you are looking for evidence of a self-destruct mechanism in Edmonds' make-up, you can do no better than to turn to the Test match against New Zealand in 1983. Once again, Edmonds had 'managed to embarrass the blighters into picking me', by taking stacks of wickets round the counties. Once again, Edmonds had been given a last chance. The feeling was divided: 'let's hope he can behave himself for once, and let's watch to see if he steps out of line so we can get rid of him once and for all'.

The captain was Bob Willis, a Brearley disciple, and no Edmonds fan. Also a man who believes that a spin bowler's principle function is to keep things tight while the seamers have a blow. Willis is a straightforward soul. And though he changed his name by deed poll to Robert George Dylan Willis, by the time he was England captain he was an establishment man through and through. He already preferred Wagner to Bob Dylan. He had no time for mavericks: they are alien to his temperament and to the seriousness with which he takes cricket.

This was the time when England was attempting to control aggressive short-pitched bowling by captains' agreements. The idea was that opposing captains were asked to agree to a limit of one bouncer per over. Funnily enough, the West Indians didn't go along with this notion. By another of those odd little quirks, New Zealand leapt at it avidly. The fact that they had only one bowler capable of delivering a decent bouncer, while England had several, might possibly have had something to do with it.

Richard Hadlee, that splendid cricketer, was the man in question. He is not only a terrific quick bowler, but also an aggressive batsman whose double of 1,000 runs and 100 wickets in 1984 surprised nobody. As a batsman he is a hitter and is one of the legion of fast bowlers who, in the immortal words of Corporal Jones, 'don't like it up 'em, sir'. Willis put Edmonds on to bowl at him. This didn't please Edmonds at all: he thought the quicks were far more likely to get Hadlee out, and maybe felt that Willis was wary of getting slogged himself.

Edmonds sees Hadlee as a hitter, and accordingly wanted an in-out field for him: a cluster round the bat and a couple on the boundary. Long on and long off are attacking positions for a slow bowler if he wants to think in that way. But Willis refused, and gave him mid on and mid off saving the one. Hadlee jovially clouted Edmonds straight over the infield for four, and then did it again: this, thought Hadlee, was the life. Edmonds' response was bizarre – indeed, brilliant, if you like that sort of thing. Off five paces, he bowled a bouncer. It rose steeply, got throat-high, and Hadlee jerked his head back in amazement. Edmonds is a strong man who knows how to use his strength, and he has a mighty left arm. He had used the bouncer as a surprise weapon before. Well, why not?

'He could have maimed Bob Taylor,' said Willis, still annoyed at the incident. It would have been polite to tell Taylor it was coming, even though Edmonds adds: 'Taylor was supposed to be the best keeper in the world, wasn't he?'

So far fair enough, if a little rough on Taylor. It disconcerted the batsman as well as the captain and the wicket-keeper, and, as Edmonds rightly says, there is often too much seriousness in cricket. There was a pleasure to take in the unconventional use of the bouncer. But if Edmonds showed his love of the bizarre with the bouncer, he showed his utter recklessness with the next ball. It was another nose-high bouncer. I remember saying to Edmonds: 'I can see the value in a spinner's bouncer as a surprise weapon . . .' Edmonds interrupted: 'You wouldn't believe how surprised he was at the second!' So was everybody else, including the umpire who, under the terms of the captains' agreement, had to call a no ball. It was a remarkable incident, but the most remarkable thing about it was that Edmonds did not bowl a third bouncer.

Of course, Willis took him off, and Edmonds finished the innings, and match, with 1 for 101. Yippee, thought the selectors: now we can drop Edmonds. He helped them out by having a back problem, missing a match, and after that, the next couple of Tests couldn't have been happier occasions for the Edmonds-haters of the world. They drafted in Nick Cook of Leicestershire, and he had the dizzying good fortune to bowl on two successive turners. Cook had an absolutely glorious time, and ended up with 17 wickets. So of course there was no need to take Edmonds on the tour to New Zealand and Pakistan that winter, since England already had a match-winning slow left-armer. Edmonds finished the season with 92 wickets at 21.45 and Cook with 73 at 25.46. Cook went on tour: Edmonds stayed at home to wheel and deal in the business world, and that, it seemed, was the final ignominious episode of Edmonds' international career. The two crazy bouncers had seen to that.

It seemed that the very last chance had been comprehensively blown. Time and again Edmonds has been given the elbow: time and again his talent has brought him back. Time and again his unerring knack of getting up the nostrils of the mighty has betrayed him. So much so that the mighty have become sensitive to the least little step out of line, seeing in a word, in a gesture, a world of defiance. It was in this way that Edmonds became involved in one of the most famous sledging rows in cricket. Sledging is the systematic abuse of batsmen, done for the sole purpose of talking them out. And Edmonds, people assume, is the gamesman supreme, never missing a trick to unsettle an opponent, playing his cricket in a bitter, moody way with personal gain his only end. This is not wholly accurate. 'Play up and play the game,' he says. 'How else can you approach cricket?' But Bob Taylor, in his book *Standing Up, Standing Back*, lays the blame for the sledging incident wholly on Edmonds.

It happened in the 1982 Test series against India. Taylor writes: 'He should have realised he was on trial under the captaincy of Bob Willis, a man who had little time for him. He had been selected this time because Derek Underwood was, like his colleagues from the South African Breweries XI, serving his three years suspension. It was another last chance. That didn't stop Phil from giving some verbals to Dilip Vengsarkar in the first Test at Lord's . . . Vengsarkar threw down his helmet and stepped away from the wicket after Phil had been trying to gee every one up; Phil then lobbed in a few unsavoury words. That was wrong, it was gamesmanship and I can't understand why he felt he had to do it. He got a rocket from Peter May, the new chairman of selectors, and was dropped after three Tests.'

To this day, Edmonds denies the story. One must remember that Taylor was 20 yards away at the time. Edmonds quite often does a little hand-clapping and exhortation of his colleagues, as does Botham and, indeed, did Taylor. David Gower, not one of your noisy captains, appreciates this. 'In a way, I wish every one was like that,' he said. 'I can't do it all the time, and it is good to have people involved and encouraging to provide the aggression and fire that unsettles batsmen. He and Both do that all right, and it is good to see. I'm not naturally aggressive in that way. His encouraging is part of the way a team works.' And with Willis going into one of his mid on trances, there was a need to keep concentration going around the bat. So much for the 'geeing up'. The sledging of Vengsarkar is a different matter, and quite unforgivable. Except, says Edmonds, it didn't actually happen. Wearily, reluctant to dredge up yet another old row, Edmonds said: 'I'm the nicest guy in the world on the field. I'd been having a laugh with Vengsarkar in the nets, and then, when he came out to bat at Lord's, he was very nervous. The Indians on the balcony decided that I was standing too close. Vengsarkar was looking very agitated, and I said to him: "Never mind, Dilip, it's only a Test match." I can only assume that he didn't hear what I was saying. Helmets do block your hearing. And because he was nervous, he totally over-reacted. So all at once I'm the great sledger. People believe what they want to believe, don't they?'

All the same, to get involved in the incident at all was unfortunate, and Edmonds has a knack of getting involved in unfortunate incidents. To get involved in that one, when on trial, was doubly unfortunate – in fact it was a complete error of judgement, which brings us back to the classic Edmonds cry: 'I've been so stupid and naïve. I'm so naïve its unbelievable!'

'He's always telling us how naïve he is,' said the roundly impressed Willis. 'A guy who wheels and deals like him can't possibly be as naïve as he claims.' But Willis ignored the streak of recklessness with which Edmonds can be consumed in a trice. If Edmonds were a gunman he would always shoot from the hip even if he remembered to make his opponent stand with the sun in his eyes.

It is genuine recklessness that characterises Edmonds, not a mean streak. The bitter sledging that was the hallmark of the Australian team of the seventies, and which other teams and individuals have also followed, is not something Edmonds admires. 'You hear so much bullshit talked about winning and losing. Of course when you're on the pitch you're playing hard, but it's much more important in the long run to satisfy the consumer. And you do that by playing the game like a gentleman.

100

'Very little real sledging actually goes on. Boys from the press like to imagine that it happens all the time, but to tell the truth, I have never experienced sledging. When I was batting, Tony Greig, in a good-natured way, used to tell John Snow to knock my head off as he started his run, but that's not sledging. Not to me it isn't. That's banter.

'What does go on is a lot of by-play between fielders at the batsman's expense. Say I'm at short leg, and Clive Radley is opposite at silly point: I talk openly to him about how the next ball is coming to his right, or his left, so make sure you're ready to catch it . . . but that isn't sledging. I expect guys to do it to me when I'm batting. It can cause ill-feeling occasionally, but I enjoy it – on the receiving end, I mean. The Indians are great at it. Sivaramakrishnan's telling me: "I'm going to get you with my googly, Phil." And I'm saying: "Don't be silly, I can spot your googly miles away." Or Vengsarkar, who's always at it, saying from close in: "I'm waiting for you, I'm waiting for you!" I love it – and it's not sledging. It's give and take, and it's part of the enjoyment of competing out there. In the same way, Botham will shout "You lucky bastard!" at batsmen, when he passes the bat without them getting a touch.

'I've been told that Glenn Turner was the butt of a lot of real sledging in Australia, particularly from the Chappells. He was abused about his Indian wife and all that type of thing. I would never do that. It's ridiculous. I don't know what could have brought it on. There must have been something about Glenn's personality that attracted it.

'But I've toured in Australia, where you'd go out for a good night with Dennis Lillee and Co, and when they come along with the banter the next morning in the middle, it's just not something to take seriously. They don't take it seriously themselves.'

However, the sledging incident has mercifully been put on one side. This does not alter Edmonds' uncanny affinity with trouble. He can cause trouble from the most unpromising of circumstances: it is partly of the way of Edmonds and partly of the way of authority. There are certain people who always get stopped by gatemen even when they have the right pass – I know, I'm one of them. Edmonds has a similar problem: even now, when he is more or less accepted as part of the England set-up, he retains his knack of doing extraordinary things – or perhaps of doing things that look particularly extraordinary because it is Edmonds doing them. Edmonds, remember, is one of the few cricketers who actually like going to meet people in sponsors' tents at cricket matches. So at The Oval Test in the summer of 1985, he naturally decided to stroll round to chat in the sponsor's tent during lunch. He wanted to see people from Johnnie Walker, who had (because of their connection with Edmonds) supplied the England team with Scotch during the winter's tour of India. Edmonds being Edmonds, he went directly to the sponsor's tent, without passing Go. That involved taking a short cut across the middle of the playing area. Perfectly practical, and any one who knows anything about the gatemen at cricket grounds would give long odds against his being allowed back into the pavilion to go out and bowl in the afternoon, were he to go the public way. At the end of the lunch interval, Edmonds learned that one of the public relations girls also needed to get to the opposite side of the ground, so Edmonds gallantly offered to escort her the quick way. That gave great pleasure to the announcer, Alan Curtis, who saw a golden chance for one of his little jokes. When reading out Edmonds' figures, he added that these 'did not include the maiden he escorted during the lunch interval'. Ho ho.

But Peter May, chairman of the selectors, and Donald Carr, secretary of the Test and County Cricket Board, were not amused by Edmonds' breach of convention. They later confronted Edmonds, and May said: 'I gather you walked across the pitch at lunch time.' Edmonds laughed and agreed. 'For what reason?' 'No reason,' said Edmonds, laughing again. The matter was discussed for ten minutes, and for all that time he really thought they were joking. And then he realised they weren't, and he started laughing again, and said: 'You cannot be serious!' It is very hard to give some one a bollocking when they can't take it seriously. But it still went on, for literally ten minutes, until other people came in. So finally Peter May said: 'Well, you got Allan Border out, so we'll forgive you this time.'

Edmonds sighed, and then added thoughtfully, perceptively: 'I suppose it's not the done thing to walk across the pitch in the middle of a Test match. Why not, I wonder? Still, I expect if I was in charge, I would think exactly the same thing, and support the traditions.'

Edmonds is not only a person who likes confrontation. He is also a person people like to confront. This is why the duel between

Edmonds and Border was one of the highlights of the 1985 Ashes series, and why Border tried to smash Edmonds out of the attack as a policy of total confrontation, and got himself stumped silly. But Edmonds' confrontations – not all engineered by him – won him few victories when he captained Middlesex.

Edmonds was vice-captain of Middlesex for the 1980 and 1981 seasons. The first one hardly counts, since Brearley was in charge at Middlesex and Botham was leading England. The 1981 season was a different matter. As every cricket follower knows, this was the *annus mirabilis*. Botham gave up the captaincy about six inches ahead of the boot, so Brearley took over, and presided over Botham's subsequent miracles. Which left Edmonds captaining Middlesex in Brearley's absence.

Brearley writes, in what Frances calls 'that book of ex cathedra pronouncements', *The Art of Captaincy*: 'Vice-captains are often chosen, then, with an eye to the future. In all cases, one hopes that the person will develop and win the confidence of the side. In certain circumstances, however, one may suspect that the opposite will occur, and yet feel that it is essential to make the appointment. At its most cynical, such a move consists of giving a man enough rope to hang himself before he has too much power.' He was writing this, he adds, with Edmonds and Geoffrey Boycott in mind.

Edmonds finds this statement outrageous, and wondered if it might form the basis of a libel action. (If so he will be able to sue me as well for repeating it.) He said: 'Brearley is held with such high regard throughout England because of his cricket. So any managing director could read that, and decide at once that he would never want to do any business with a chap like Edmonds. Edmonds is not management material, look at what Brearley says. I think the paragraph is vicious, vindictive stuff. I'm not vice-captaincy material just because I don't get on with the guy?'

The 1981 Edmonds caretaker captaincy included two rows and a general atmosphere of suspicion. As said earlier, Edmonds was suspected of a devious search for personal glory by trying to bowl on wearing pitches. Edmonds always wanted to bat first. Now, there are certain cricketers who always prefer to field first. These are opening batsmen and opening bowlers. An opening batsman looks at every pitch through green-tinted spectacles. An opening batsman who is captain will tend to choose to field first at the least sign of lushness on the wicket. And Middlesex were used to having an opening batsman as captain. Seam bowlers too, want to field so they can exploit every smidgeon of damp in the wicket before the first lunch interval douses any fire the pitch may have. Conspicuous among this breed was Mike Selvey. Edmonds said: 'He was at the end of his career, and needed what help any pitch could give him: if he was going to be effective at all, it was on the first morning. Naturally he wanted to field. But I believe in the old adage that if you win the toss you think about fielding and ninety-nine times out of a hundred, you bat. Brears naturally followed a different line.'

Captains can live with unpopularity. It is part of the job. But Edmonds also managed a pair of memorable rows. In neither of them was he fully blameworthy, but there you go: he was Edmonds, and he was captain, and the cock-ups demonstrably occurred. Both of them, for some reason, involved Wayne Daniel, who, as an arch-banterer, has always been one of Edmonds' better dressing-room mates.

The first occurred at The Oval. At the time there was a rule in force by which, if a bowler left the field for more than 20 minutes, he could not bowl again for the length of time he had been off. Less than 20 minutes, and he could bowl straight away. Edmonds was captaining an attack that comprised Daniel, Selvey, Dermott Monteith and himself. 'We were getting smashed all over the park,' Edmonds said. 'Wayne had gone off, ostensibly to go to the bog. After 15 minutes, I signalled to the pavilion for him to come back on. After 19 minutes, he's nowhere to be seen. Then after about 25 minutes, he strolls back out again. No one said much till Roger Knight, the Surrey captain, asked the umpire can he bowl? He's been off 25 minutes, can he bowl? The umpire would have let him, but once Knight had made the point he couldn't. So Wayne is just coming down the steps, and I go berserk. I said: "Fuck off back to the pavilion and don't come back till teatime." Yes, in front of the members. Apparently that caused much consternation, every one took offence.'

Captains have been known to harangue their players in the most opprobrious terms before, of course. Edmonds himself has been upbraided before the members in full four-letter terms by Mike

Gatting. But this one went down badly, the story 'Edmonds sent Wayne Daniel off the field' sounded too much like an outrageous Edmonds story to be forgotten lightly. Various people were waiting with touching eagerness for Edmonds to step out of line: how typical of Edmonds, then, to give them something to go on. Again, Edmonds had acted with recklessness.

The other Edmonds-Daniel affair cost Middlesex a championship win. It happened in a match against Sussex at Brighton, and there was a doubt about Daniel's fitness. 'Now I'm a pretty straightforward guy. If you say you're fit when I ask, I assume you're fit. The wicket looked as if it would turn a bit. I went to the wicket with Clive Radley, and Mike Sturt the Middlesex chairman of selectors, and we agreed that the thing to do was to leave out Mike Selvey, since Wayne had told me he was fit. Fine. So what happens? Wayne breaks down in the first innings. We are left with an attack of Simon Hughes, Monteith and me. A little thin, wouldn't you say? We got slaughtered. Imran Khan rushed in and bowled at the speed of light, we had no one to counter – and the captain has to take responsibility. No one else counts. We got slaughtered and that's it.'

It is, no doubt, unfair that Edmonds had to bear the responsibility. But there are enough times when some blunder or other ends up looking like inspired captaincy, and all the captain can do then is grin sheepishly and take all the credit. On this occasion, it didn't work out that way. Daniel was at fault in declaring himself fit to play. Edmonds was unlucky, and captains are not paid to be unlucky. As Richie Benaud said: 'Captaincy is 90 per cent luck and 10 per cent skill . . . but for heaven's sake don't try it without that little 10 per cent.' But the fact remains that if people were genuinely looking for reasons to nudge Edmonds out of the vice-captaincy, Edmonds had given them something to work on.

And so Edmonds was replaced by Mike Gatting as vice-captain for Brearley's final year in charge, the 1982 season. Gatting succeeded to the captaincy the following year and won the Benson and Hedges Cup, and followed with the NatWest Trophy in 1984 and the championship in 1985. It could have been Edmonds. Or perhaps not.

It could also have been John Emburey. He might well have got the vice-captaincy ahead of Gatting, when Edmonds was sacked. Emburey was passed over. Apparently, at a Middlesex committee meeting he did not disclose that his departure to South Africa was imminent. (He left the next day.) Subsequently, he was later made vice-captain when Gatting became captain.

CHAPTER 9

THE DILETTANTE ENTREPRENEUR

Edmonds is not just a professional cricketer. He is also a professional businessman – 'a dealer and dilettante entrepreneur' is his own description. He was probably born scheming. He is like the Michael Caine character who, as heads drop all around him, says inevitably: 'Look – I've got a great idea!' Edmonds has always got a great idea for the next project – more usually, he has half-a-dozen great ideas on the go at the same time. But combining his ambitions of being a hotshot entrepreneur with his still unfulfilled cricketing career is never a straightforward matter. Take the time he was trying to buy a hotel for an Arab consortium.

Edmonds had met the Galladari family when he was in Dubai, through the family's involvement with the Dubai Cricket Association. As usual, while most of the cricketers were bored with 'ear-bashing', Edmonds revelled in the chance to talk to the powerful businessmen of Dubai. He talked long and hard with members of the Galladari family, and, Edmonds being Edmonds and the Galladaris being Galladaris, the subject was naturally business. The encounter left behind a definite feeling on both sides that business should be done together in the future. Later on the chance came: the Galladaris had ambitions of buying a hotel in London. So they asked Edmonds to be their middleman – on a percentage basis, naturally. Some people like to work for a flat fee, but Edmonds would always prefer to work for the chance of making a lot if the deal comes off, and take the chance of getting nothing if it does not. It was a good idea from the Galladaris' point of view. They knew Edmonds had a great deal of business nous, they knew he was good talker, they knew that many top business-men would be eager to take a call from Phil Edmonds. And above all, they knew no one would connect a cricketer with Arab money – and the first whiff of Arab interest would hit the price for six.

It all happened in the middle of the English cricket-season, when Edmonds was, naturally, playing seven days a week. He was compelled, then, to make all his business calls from dressing-room payphones. So there was Edmonds, in his flannels, talking things through to the hoteliers: 'Yes my clients are happy to do business. The price they are talking about is seven million poun – ' Poo-poo-poo went the payphone, leaving Edmonds scrabbling desperately for a 10p piece. He got cut off, and had to borrow a coin from a Middlesex team-mate before trying again to discuss the multi-million pound deal.

Business is a fascination for Edmonds. He is unendingly grateful that cricket has given him the chance to meet so many men of power. Talking business with the top men in the profession is a constant source of education, and the making of contacts some-times opens the way for a chance to set up a venture. Leading city businessmen go to sponsors' tents in England: top politicians and men of business attend all the 'ear-bashing' cocktail parties on tours. Even if there were no chance of personal advantage from such meetings, Edmonds would revel in them: success fascinates him and he could sit and look at it for hours. 'People who have reached the top of their own profession are often interested in meeting those who have reached the top in another,' Edmonds said. Ian Botham has his friendships with Mick Jagger and Elton John: Edmonds hobnobs with men of financial and political clout. In each case, the interest is a two-way thing. Vic Marks says, in his book on the 1984–85 tour, *Marks out of XI*, that you could always tell who was the most important man in the room, because Edmonds would be talking to him. Edmonds acknowledges that there is truth in this, though it would be a mistake to judge this habit in crude what's-in-it-for-me terms. He is genuinely fascinated by men of power, and what is more, can talk to them on equal terms. Edmonds has a reputation for awkwardness, but he is also a man of immense charm. He can talk sharply and amusingly: he has the unconscious knack of being extremely impressive. Furthermore, the most flattering thing in the world is to have someone you admire showing a great interest in you. Edmonds is not only a palpably admirable cricketer but one who takes a genuine interest in people whom most cricketers find deathly dull.

Edmonds' business interests, however, do set him further apart from his cricketing colleagues. Not only is Edmonds rather cagey when discussing his business involvements, but also in England, men of business are mistrusted. In the United States, the middle classes can't wait to tell you about their share portfolios: in Hong Kong typists and office boys sprint across the road when the closing prices on the stock exchange go up outside the banks. But most Englishmen see business as something alien: a kind of white man's magic. To read the *Financial Times* is to declare yourself as a man apart – certainly in a cricket dressing-room.

'But to tell the truth, I have been a complete dilettante on the business side,' Edmonds insists. His interests, however, have been wide-ranging. Property tops the list, of course, but other projects that stick in the mind as having the unmistakable Edmonds stamp include an abattoir and a gold mine. He has also been involved in a number of cricketing deals. 'For years the only sponsorship deals at Middlesex were done by me,' he said. 'The mistake I made, of course, was doing it all for free. Had I charged the lads 50 per cent as their PR manager, they would have been grateful to me. As it was, they all assumed I had an ulterior motive. And when I stopped setting up deals for them, they all said what a selfish fellow I was, not doing anything for them.' Edmonds was instrumental in setting up Middlesex's sponsorship by Austin Reed; he has helped the club set up sponsored cars, boots and cleaning. He even managed to persuade Johnnie Walker to provide the England touring team in India with enormous quantities of Scotch – which was doubly generous of him, since he doesn't actually drink the stuff. His benefit, characteristically, was a precision planned affair: none of the optimistic bumbling round pubs for Edmonds.

It is not his style: he is the type who always thinks big. 'Thinking in millions simplifies the arithmetic no end,' he said. Frances said: 'I hear Phil talking in millions on the telephone while I am

109

wondering how I am going to pay the electricity bill. I don't know what the Middlesex players think when they hear him discussing millions on the dressing-room payphone.' In fact, Edmonds does his best not to talk business when he is surrounded by people who are wondering how they are going to make their £10,000 season's pay last out through the winter.

'People sometimes wonder how someone with my temperament was content to play county cricket for so long, when there seemed to be no chance of getting back into the England set-up. Frances wanted me to retire, she wanted me to retire very early on and become a merchant banker. But there are lots of reasons why I carried on playing cricket. One of these is that cricket is only one part of my life: and when my cricket was at its lowest ebb, the excitement of doing business kept me going. And in just the same way, cricket has kept me optimistic when I have been disappointed in business.

'Business-wise I spend a lot of time trying to set up projects, and most of the time, they don't come off. You expect that. When one deal does come off, you know what you have been working for through all the disappointments. I do my real work when I am not playing cricket. And even when the deals don't come off, they are fascinating. I get the same buzz from trying to set up a deal as I do bowling to Allan Border. Participation is the important thing, being right at the heart of the action – not fielding on the third man boundary, as it were.

'This is also the reason why I have so far been just a dilettante in business. I sometimes regret leaving the firm of chartered surveyors, Edward Erdman. If I had stayed with them, I would have had a lot more experience in property and finance – and it is still in property that my major business interests lie, property and land. As Mark Twain said, "invest in land, son. They ain't making it any more".'

But if property is his most considerable interest, he has no objection to involving himself in those jugglings of paper and finances that baffle those without financial brains. It was through just such a deal that he became involved with Kerry Packer. 'It was the start of various machinations in the oil business in the States – a series of transactions which culminated, much later, in Texaco being sued to the tune of 11 billion dollars by Penzoil Corporation. A friend of mine had lined up a substantial credit facility for the takeover of a major American oil company – and there were billions involved. Everything checked out and looked feasible, including the timing. The chances of making a few bucks looked very good, so I decided to phone Kerry Packer, who I thought might be interested. I had met him, but I can hardly say I knew him well or was at all close. I rang up Tony Greig who works for him in Australia, and said I wanted to speak to Kerry. Kerry called me back in the morning, and I explained the situation to him, and my thoughts on it. He asked how much I wanted. I said, a 50–50 split. He said no – his American funding man needed a share: a third each. He said he was interested in taking $6 million worth of shares. So we talked a little about business generally, and then he said, OK, never mind, I'll take the lot – $7.5 million worth of shares. On Tuesday, the money was there: all $7.5 million. Everything was hunkydory. I thought it was all going to go: and I was on for a potential third of the profit – a potential third of $5 million. But somehow, things got slow, and didn't happen when they should have happened – and Kerry gave me a deadline of a week: still things didn't happen, and so he pulled out. I expect I have lost a great deal of credibility in his eyes because of that. Unfortunately the timing was slightly wrong, and the deal went through a short while later.

'When people talk about Kerry Packer, particularly people from the cricket establishment, they say things like: "Oh, you can't trust the man." But I know what I know. On the basis of a half-hour phone conversation he promised millions of bucks, and what's more, he was as good as his word.

'Obviously, I was sorry when the deal aborted. But it had been an exciting few weeks – and of course, it wasn't the end of everything, because I had my cricket to go back to. On the other hand, this is something that works the other way: because of the cricket, I can't always do the business deals I had hoped for. In terms of fulfilling myself as a cricketer, it was great to go on the tour of India in 1984. But from a pure business angle, the opportunity cost was enormous. Various plans connected with Business Expansion Scheme projects had to be postponed and subsequently aborted. I also had some plans connected with central London residential accommodation and property in France. Because I was in India, I missed the boat. But then England won the series, and the Ashes the following summer – and it was nice to take part!'

Edmonds has been interested and involved in business as long as he can remember. It is something of a family trait. As Redgraves are born acting, so Edmondses are born dealers. Agile-brained and light on his feet, he will always have a great idea or two, and a list of contacts to whom he will suggest them – contacts he will mostly have made through playing cricket. Business is an attitude of mind: a distinct method of attacking life. Evenings at the Edmonds home are wont to be interrupted by long phone calls about, say, setting up satellite receiving dishes on pubs so that they can show exclusive overseas cricket to their clients. Going out for a drink with Edmonds will see him stopping to check estate agents' windows so he can monitor the rents local landlords are asking.

'If I hadn't been a cricketer, I suppose I would now be a successful property man, right up there in the top echelon,' Edmonds said. 'Right now, I'm a wheeler-dealer in a dilettantish sort of way. Other cricketers find that amazing – but the thing that amazes me is that the cricket deals I do for myself aren't nearly as ruthless as other guys manage. I seem to have very little idea of my own value as a cricketer, and am not nearly as hard in negotiating personal terms as other guys are.'

Frances put her finger on this phenomenon: 'By and large, Phil's colleagues are cricketers, and cricketers only. They only have half a life, a few years at the top. They know that they have *got* to screw all they can from cricket in the years they are at the top. But Phil doesn't need to put all his energies into screwing the last dollar from cricket, because he has always seen cricket as a transitional phase – a very long transition, true, but he still has as much life outside as inside cricket. He works twice as hard when he is not playing cricket.' 'My real work days are my days off from cricket,' Edmonds said.

'You don't need to screw your cricket deals until the pips squeak,' Frances said. Edmonds agreed: 'I'm sure I don't get the best I could from cricket. In fact, I know I am being conned most of the time – but I still go along with it.'

Of course, since Packer turned the game upside down, players get more chance of making money from mere cricket than ever before: top cricketers everywhere have done better. England men get £1,500 for a home Test match, for example. And with cricket being so popular at the moment, entrepreneurs are eager to offer top players commercial opportunities. Botham's commercial ventures ('Attack with Botham trousers!'), and his long-term ambitions to go

112

to Hollywood and be Biggles or Raffles, are well known. Botham will not become one of those sad stars of former days whose only joy is the past. Botham's former agent, Tim Hudson, once told me: 'Mr Botham has decided that it is time he grew up. He has the choice – he can be Freddie Trueman, or he can become an international figure like Arnold Palmer.' David Gower, too, has a good share of commercial interests, which include representing a fine porcelain company, which is, one must admit, a very Goweresque venture.

But for your average county pro, the reward for years of association with the game is The Benefit. The benefit system is something that Edmonds feels very much in two minds about. 'There is no denying the fact that it is legalised begging,' he said. 'And it is the most insidious institution in cricket. Another reason why I never left Middlesex, to take up the captaincy somewhere else, was because like so many cricketers, I got caught in the benefit rut. Often there comes a time when you want to leave – when leaving might be the right thing to do for every reason. But you know that if you stay on for two or three years more, it will be your turn for a benefit, your turn to make a substantial sum of money – and all tax-free.' Jack Simmons, stalwart servant of Lancashire as well as a splendid fellow, made £128,000 from his benefit. In 1984, Geoff Boycott, a totem figure if ever there was one, made £147,954.

'The benefit system allows counties to buy loyalty without spending a cent,' Edmonds said. 'It is the way in which you are finally rewarded for working for years for a pittance. I suppose you could see it as an enforced savings scheme.' Edmonds, understandably, did not let any misgivings about the value of the benefit system inhibit him when it came to collecting his own due reward for years of service in 1983. His committee did well. They even persuaded Saatchi and Saatchi not only to give him some advice, but also to sponsor him for every wicket he took in the season. His benefit brochure had a circulation of more than one million copies guaranteed – because it was a supplement to the entire range of IPC boys' comics. 'There is definitely big money to be made in publishing if one has the time,' he said. With his committee he also invented a new concept for raking in the loot, a scheme that is now standard practice for beneficiaries: six-a-side company cricket tournaments. 'They initiated the whole six-a-side pro-am concept,' Edmonds said. 'It seemed a good idea, and I was convinced it would work. I know lots of companies as well as lots of cricketers – and everybody loves to mix with the stars.' In truth, the idea of mixing with the stars is what makes most benefits work. Attending pubs to draw raffles for autographed bats, depends for its money-making on the beneficiary's presence in the pub. Edmonds, however, put the concept on the most rational basis yet seen: a dozen companies are each invited, for a donation, to put out a side of five players, and each side is led by a professional cricketer. The pros will obviously give their services free, on the mutual back-scratching basis that is also a central part of the benefit business.

'I had a complete week in which I had a six-a-side competition every day,' Edmonds said. 'Each day, I had a different sector of the market down to play. I had a liquor companies day, when 12 liquor companies each put out a side. I had a computer day, a stock-brokers day, and I had a bookmakers day sponsored by one company. They all brought their clients, mixed with the stars, cheered their team, and had a good time, and I did very well indeed from it. It is exactly the right package: with six-a-side you get a lot of matches in the day, and since everybody has to bowl an over in every match, every one is involved. If you have two pitches, as at Uxbridge, you can get 12 companies along at £1,000 a time. That's £12,000 in a day: big money even after you have paid your expenses.

'My committee concentrated on companies, rather than individuals, throughout my benefit. When I had benefit dinners, I didn't try to sell single tickets to individuals: I rang up people I knew in companies and offered them the whole table of 10 places. Simple as that. To sell 10 individuals would take all week.

'So I was fortunate to make a fair whack from my benefit – it was easily a Middlesex record. I owe Middlesex something for that. I know that people had feared I would walk out as soon as my benefit was finished. But you can't do things like that.'

Edmonds, with his interests in both commerce and cricket, is a great believer in the power of each party to help the other. He wants to see Middlesex do far more to encourage executive entertainment at mere county games: 'A leisurely day at county cricket is the ideal background for a little low-pressure selling,' he said. 'Particularly with the guaranteed attendance of the players. Everyone loves the chance to say, "well done on bowling Allan Border, and was it an arm ball that got him?"' Edmonds goes further than that. He believes that companies could profitably pursue a far closer relationship with the counties.

'I'm talking about old-fashioned patronage. A system in which players could be sponsored by a firm, and could actually work for that firm during the winter – and earn their money, too! In this way, they would have a career waiting for them at the end of their playing days. It would do away with so much of the terrible insecurity of the average pro's existence. The system has worked for years in India, and there is no reason why it should not work here. For all but a few at the top, cricket is one of the most insecure jobs you can have: the problem of what you do when you are forced to quit at 35 or whatever is, for many people, a terrible one. The patronage system would ease that problem hugely, and, because you have been working for the firm in your winters, you would have a natural, easy transition from cricket to the real world. For many cricketers, it is adjusting to a life outside cricket that is particularly hard. And the company would do well from this in many ways.

'As I said, business is an attitude of mind, an approach to life, and if you are a business-minded fellow involved in cricket, it is natural to come up with notions for combining the two: "Look – I've got a great idea."' The best ideas are always the simple ones, but naturally, it takes a nimble brain to see them, and to make them happen. An example of Edmonds' adroitness is his notion to take advantage of all the exposure of cricket on TV.

'There are 270 hours of cricket on television every year. The prime area of concentration is the pitch: and the one thing you are looking at practically all the time is the bat. So that makes a bat the ideal place for an advertisement. Of course, the BBC and the TCCB wouldn't let you go to the wicket with a bat that said "Buy Blogg's Beer" all over it. But the bat manufacturers like Gunn and Moore, or Duncan Fearnley all have their own logos on bats, and they are very clearly visible on the television for hour after hour. Now obviously, it would be great to have your own company logo on a cricket bat, no matter what kind of company you were. Say you had a really identifiable logo, like the Shell symbol, on a bat. Every time you saw Botham hitting a six, the message coming through would be "Buy Shell". Well, the BBC and the TCCB say there would be no objection to this at all – provided that Shell were bona-fide bat

115

manufacturers, and you could go to the sports shop and buy a Shell bat to use on the village green. The point is that it would be brilliant exposure for the entire Shell company – almost like subliminal advertising.

'Well, I have a company that is very interested in the notion, and with them, I am negotiating to take over a bat manufacturing company. A company that would go on making bats and selling them, but instead of buying it under the old name, the club players would be buying, say, a Phil Edmonds/Shell bat, or whatever. And the professionals would all be playing with Shell bats: and they would be promoting an entire major company instead of a little bat-making concern. I am deep in the negotiations – and as usual, I am optimistic.'

Edmonds will often speak of cricket as a money-making concern, which some might find a little cynical of him. But in terms of the strictest and least romantic realism, what any money-making concern must do is satisfy the consumer. In such terms, it is the old pro types, with their seeking of grinding victories, time-wasting and stubborn draws, that are the impractical romantics here. Edmonds says: 'To attract the consumer to cricket, you must play the game like a gentleman. Of course you are playing hard, and playing to win: but in the long-term interests of the game and its players, it is far more important to satisfy the consumer than it is to win.

'The most obvious example of the way in which cricketers lose the sympathy of the consumer is over the matter of bad light. There really must be radical changes here. Often the idea of coming off for light is nonsensical. When you are out there, you get used to the light.' Indeed, many a club cricketer has faced swiftish bowling while cars have been passing the ground with their headlights on. And they are playing for fun, not to entertain people. 'People say, if the guy gets out, the one that comes in is in danger, because he is not used to the light. Well, that is just a fact of life, and one cricketers must get used to. Nothing angers the paying customer more than to be cheated of his money's worth by people coming off for bad light. We need these people on our side, we need them to come again and again to the cricket – and so as part of the marketing of the game, we should not come off for marginal light. Players must accept that – and play on.'

I could practically hear the 'hear, hears' of frustrated cricket watchers across the country as Edmonds said this. He is a great believer in giving and receiving value, and he believes that if cricket is to market itself properly, giving value is the first essential. That cricketers should willingly take trouble to meet the businessmen in the sponsors' tents, is of course a central part of this: he knows how much people enjoy meeting cricketers. 'That is why when I am in the City to meet people, I will generally wear a cricket blazer.' I accused him of 'dressing-up as a cricketer': 'Well, you must face the fact that I *am* a cricketer. And it helps to break the ice at meetings: people ask what badge was that? And I say, the tour of India badge, so they ask how I enjoyed the tour, and so on. Sometimes, however, I make an appointment with a guy to make a business proposition, and he agrees to the meeting so that he can talk to me about cricket, when he doesn't want to do business at all. But there's no getting away from the fact that being a cricketer has given me some matchless opportunities for meeting people – and I'm not just talking about businessmen. That is not only interesting. It is very, very useful.

'I remember when I was touring Grenada in 1974 with a Derek Robbins XI. We met the then premier, Sir Eric Gairy: he was in his full regalia – a morning suit and a massive chain of office – and he greeted us at this typical cocktail party. I got talking to him, of course, as Vic Marks would expect, Sir Eric being the most important man in the room. And he invited me to bring some of the team along to his discotheque the following evening. So I thought, fine, and a bunch of us went to his place the next day. It was called The Rock Garden, and who was there collecting the admission money at the entrance, but Sir Eric Gairy – wearing a psychedelic jacket, neckerchief, and Polaroid wraparound shades. I went up to him and said: 'Hi, nice to see you, Mr Prime Minister. Thank you for inviting us.' But he seemed a bit flummoxed. We all went in and had a good time – and I thought later, maybe he was expecting us to pay all along.' However, Edmonds has the presence that can even get a dictator to stand aside.

Top cricketers naturally come against top people. Receptions at Number 10 Downing Street are no piercing novelty for an international cricketer. On tour the chances of meeting leading political and business figures are quadrupled: after Mrs Gandhi's assassination, the England squad were flown to Sri Lanka in a helicopter

117

courtesy of the Sri Lankan president, Junius Jayewardene. On the trip, Edmonds met the Sri Lankan minister for Land and Resources, who also happens to be the president of the Sri Lankan Cricket Board of Control. Because of Edmonds' own interests in land economy and management, the minister arranged for Edmonds to make a helicopter tour of many projects in the country, which fascinated him. 'India, too, was incredibly interesting, in terms of politics, business and, naturally, cricket. Some of the cricketers just think what a bore, more curry to eat. Not me. I believe that 99 times out of 100, the fellow at the top of his profession will have something about him that makes him more interesting than an ordinary man.' As a sportswriter, I endorse this sentiment entirely. I am often asked if I don't get bored with sportsmen with limited vocabularies and objectives. But people who have fought for and who have achieved excellence cannot help but be exceptional people, and it is up to the interviewer to seek what it is that makes them so. For there is no questioning the fact that being a top sportsman requires rather more than mere physical ability – in the same way that being a successful businessman needs more than the ability to add up.

That Edmonds has succeeded as a sportsman is not in doubt, after his part in the series victories over India and Australia. His skills as a businessman are also considerable – and like his cricket career, his business life has not been entirely easeful travelling. 'I have had a few successes, particularly in property,' he said. On the other hand, there is a certain flat in London worth a lot of money, that has become a scar in Edmonds' side. Every time he passes it, the wound is re-opened: 'I owned it, and I put it up as collateral for the abattoir my brother Pierre and I owned and operated. Because of a change in bank policy we decided to close down with a tiny deficit, and I had to sell the flat to pay off the debt. That doesn't look so bright, does it? The fact is the bank manager panicked, and his panic put us out of business and cost me £80,000. The thing was, the Third World debt crisis had got to the bank at top level, and caused a change of policy on the domestic front. So we went down the pan. It was a great pity – but then one has to go forward!

'The abattoir was a nice business, too, turning over half a million a year. It was a shame to close down when we had a lot of goodwill among the local farmers. The loss also persuaded us in part to alter the way we ran our farm in Kent. Pierre did the day-to-day operating, and he is a tremendous worker, with immense energy. He built up a really beautiful dairy herd, but because of the deal with the abattoir and a sudden implementation of milk quotas, we decided to rationalise. Now we rent the farmland for grazing, and rent our milk quota as well. The property is appreciating nicely, but it is not much use in terms of income. One day we'll do something good with it – turn it into a leisure park, or whatever, because the pressure on land is increasing all the time.

'But it's not easy. The thing is, cricket takes up so much time. It is expected that a top cricketer must play cricket seven days a week throughout the summer. No other country operates a system like that. I lose so much time when I could be out in the City doing deals and making money, when I'm just sitting around in a dressing room watching guys bat, or watching the rain come down and the guys playing cards. It is very frustrating.

'In an ideal world, I wouldn't be playing county cricket at all – and nor would a lot of top international cricketers. It is ridiculous to expect people like Both to play cricket seven days a week and still be fresh enough to win a few Test matches. No wonder he needed a winter off. I would love it if I could play club cricket on Saturdays, and international cricket in due season – and nothing else. Phil Edmonds of Hampstead and England. How does that sound? I could stay in cricket for years longer if that were to happen.

'A lot of leading players feel the same way, and that's why I don't think Tim Hudson's idea of a circus of top stars playing festival cricket at seaside towns throughout the summer is something to laugh off totally. He has not thought the thing through completely, but there is the germ of an idea in what he says. He thinks that county cricket should be mostly for young guys learning their trade and that after 25, if you haven't made it you might as well give up. And you can progress from there into being an international star – also playing festival cricket. It is certainly a notion that will interest a lot of the leading players.

'All the same, I am obviously very grateful to cricket in many ways. Sure, it takes up a lot of time, and Frances wishes I would retire tomorrow. But on the other hand, through cricket I have had so many opportunities to travel and make powerful contacts and through these, sometimes, some useful deals. There is no way I wish to get away from the fact: cricket gave me the opportunity.

'And yet . . . and yet . . . well, a business contact rang me up the other day, and had a proposal, and asked me to meet him the following week. "Sorry, can't do that," I said. "I'm going to Jamaica to play in Clive Lloyd's benefit." He said: "Bloody hell, Phil – you're always playing cricket! When are you going to do something serious?" '

CHAPTER 10

TEAM MAN

'I should have been a golfer,' Phil Edmonds is wont to remark. It is unlikely that he would have been a champion. His impatient and impulsive nature would surely have provoked him into attempting aggressive wallops over towering stands of trees, or majestic carries over vast stretches of open water: he is not a man that plays the percentages, nor a man capable, as a tournament pro must be, of building up a solid succession of minor placings to keep the exchequer ticking over.

'That's probably right,' Edmonds conceded. 'I only really mean it as a throwaway remark. Because there is one way in which I envy golfers – they don't have to consider ten other guys all the time.' It has been said before that the self-obsessed, technique-crazy approach to cricket adopted by Geoff Boycott would have made him a brilliant golfer. Perhaps Edmonds, with his love of attack and of confrontation as well as his boundless self-reliance, is temperamentally equipped to be a tennis player.

But instead, he has spent his sporting life bound up with a team game. Admittedly, cricket is a unique team game, in which individual confrontations are an integral part, but a professional cricketer spends most of his life depending on the performances of his team-mates, and a sizeable part of it merely watching them getting on with it.

Edmonds has an inordinately high coefficient of frustration. He is a restless fellow who cannot bear not to be doing anything. Sleep, as his room-mates know, is something he considers a waste of time. Similarly, hanging about in cricket pavilions is not his favourite activity: for Edmonds, time is for filling, not for killing. When his side is fielding, he likes to bowl a great many overs, as many as possible. When he is not bowling, he likes to field somewhere where something is always likely to happen: he does not enjoy those prolonged periods of quiet meditation down at third man that give so much pleasure to cricketers of less restless bent.

There is a touch of theatricality about his fielding. When meeting strangers, Edmonds tends to come over aloof and reserved, a rather self-conscious figure. But there is no self-consciousness about him on the cricket field: he swaggers about in a way that threatens to out-Botham Botham. He favours fielding positions where concentration is demanded, where there is much to do – and where he is clearly noticeable. He will stand crazily close at short leg. With his great domed forehead and overhanging brow, he looks the image of Brian Close recalled to cricketing life: a spectre of that recklessly courageous old termagant walking again on the cricket fields of England.

'Nobody fields as close as I do,' Edmonds said. 'For one thing, they have a lot more sense. For another, they see their cricket in a different way. I am not there simply to take catches. My presence there also makes the batsman play in a different way. It is perfectly possible for a close-in fielder to catch a good, solid defensive stroke off the face of the bat. So a batsman has to change the way he plays – I defy anybody to play the same way when I am on top of him. I am there to put pressure on him, I am doing an important job even if I never touch the ball. I might make the batsman extra cautious, or I might make him over-aggressive, trying to hit the ball harder. But when he is doing that, he is likely to be over-eager to wipe the ball, probably at me – and get himself caught behind. My name doesn't go on the scorecard, but it's a wicket that might not have fallen had I not been there.'

Inevitably Edmonds turns fielding into a matter of confrontation rather than one of retrieving balls. He has swift reactions, hands like buckets, and is surprisingly agile, considering he was the heaviest cricketer in the squad that went to the West Indies in 1986: heavier even than Mike Gatting – who was initially 30 pounds overweight. His ferocious and uncompromising attitude to fielding was a central part of England's scintillating performances in the field in the 1985 Ashes series, in which Edmonds took seven catches, some of them dazzlers. It should have been eight, but he suffered a mental aberration and dropped a simple chance at short leg – he admits that he was trying to throw it up in the air in triumph before he had got full control of it. 'He just looked at me,' David Gower said. 'Later he apologised, and we had a wry giggle over it.'

Edmonds doesn't even wear a helmet at short leg: he finds them uncomfortable. He has never been hit seriously – until his latest tour – nothing worse than rainbow bruises, at any rate. He got hit on the thigh by Allan Border in 1985, and his reaction to that was nothing less than Closeian. 'I should have dived across the pitch and caught the rebound,' he said, genuinely annoyed with himself for this slow reaction. He has been rocked back onto his heels by the blow, but to have flung himself forward and clung onto the ball at Border's feet would have satisfied both his taste for drama and his taste for confrontation in one splendid moment.

'I have had some pretty frightening moments when fielding in close,' he said. 'I remember one time when I was fielding 45 degrees behind square to Embers, who was bowling to Mike Denness. He bowled an appalling ball, a slow long-hop outside leg stump. Normally Denness would have swept it square, but this ball was so appalling, and so wide, that he picked up his bat, looked me in the eye and drilled the ball behind square. It went straight for me like a bullet, and all I could do was close my eyes. The ball hit me on the shoulder. Now I happened to be wearing three sweaters, because it was a cold day, and somehow, the ball seemed to stick to the wool for a moment before bouncing gently upwards. So I just stretched out a hand and took it: easy as you like. Denness went off practically crying in frustration, and we were laughing fit to burst.'

Edmonds feels that a further advantage of fielding close in is that it inspires the rest of the fielding side. 'At once, all the other fielders get the impression the entire team is being really aggressive: we are really pushing for something to happen. We are not waiting for something to turn up, we are really trying to force the pace.'

Edmonds argues that fielding really close in is safer than fielding semi-close. You are, he said, generally above the ball. He does not field close to slow bowlers, and he will not field close to any bowler he has, for the moment, lost faith in. 'I remember saying to Both

123

once, as I went to field in very close: "If you're going to bowl anything short, make sure it's up round the throat." But he bowled a couple of dreadful long-hops, and Border wiped them both in my direction, so I said: "OK, Both, that's enough," and moved back.'

This stuff about throat balls and intimidatory fielding upsets the romantic observers of the game: the people who believe that cricket is a gentle game played exclusively by gentlemen of the cloth bowling leg-spin. The truth is that cricket has always been a game that demands physical courage. The ball has always been hard and there have always been men capable of bowling it at lethal speeds. In the early 19th century, George Brown bowled a practice ball that went straight through a coat held out by his trembling long-stop and killed a dog that was loitering behind. Modern cricketers accept that courage and bruises are part of the game: that devastating speed and intimidating fielding are legitimate tactics. Edmonds loves to stand at short leg when the game is running hot, and, on his day, can play the quick men with competence as well as composure.

All the same, his batting record is not all that it might be. He remains the all-rounder that almost was. In the 1976 season, he scored 892 first class runs, but in 1985, his grand total was down to 221, with a highest score of 29. It is a pretty poor show from a man who has three first class centuries to his credit. In the meantime, his spinning partner John Emburey has, with a cricketer's professional canniness, turned himself from a dreadful batsman into a useful late-middle-order man, capable of accumulating runs with an unpretty nudging technique, or of slogging cheerfully and some-times effectively.

Edmonds, however, has mastered the art of getting out to practically everyone. He has thrown his wicket away on numerous occasions during the Brearley years, when his irritation at Brearley's slow batting drove the sense from his technique. When his concen-tration lapses, he can get out tamely, or take reckless swipes and fall to 'balls that Both would have knocked clean out of the ground'. All the same, Edmonds remains a splendid, clean hitter of the ball on his day, and it would be fun to see him back among the runs.

Over the years he has managed to find some original and imaginative ways of getting out. One of the best of these occurred when he was facing Derek Underwood, a confrontation that Edmonds has always enjoyed. 'I went to sweep, and missed. The ball hit my pad and bounced up over my shoulder. I thought it was going to hit the wicket, so I turned round to dab it away with the back of my bat. But I was using a scooped bat at the time, and the ball stuck in one of the scoops. It ran all the way along the groove and trickled off the end: John Shepherd dived and caught it. Everybody had a great laugh about that.

'Another time, I was batting against a fairly innocuous bowler, I can't remember who it was, but I was well on top of him at the time. I hit the ball straight back, very hard indeed. Fred Titmus was batting at the other end, doing nothing, when the ball hit the handle of his bat and ricocheted up in the air. Mid-off took the catch without any trouble whatsoever. Thanks Fred, I said. I was in the middle of a bad trot at the time, so you can imagine how annoying it was.'

However, in the 1985 season, Edmonds' batting deteriorated to such an extent that if he got much lower in the order he would need a designated hitter, as a pitcher does in baseball. 'I know I should have made more of my batting,' he said. 'But too often my good resolutions disappear when I'm out there in the middle. I hit a four, so I want to hit another four – so I get out. Partly, the problem is concentration. And partly, it is because I don't have the mental ability that old pros seem to acquire, to keep myself and my average firmly in mind at all times. These guys learn to cash in when the bowling is weak, and on those occasions I am likely to get out by trying to hit the cover off the ball. They also learn to hang on in there picking up runs when the going is tough and the bowlers are on top. I have tremendous respect for one old pro I know, who I am convinced is totally chicken. Really frightened of fast bowling. If he is playing against a side with a West Indian quick, and he has scored 50 or 60 in the first innings, there is no way he is going to hang around in the middle. But if he has failed in the first innings, he will skip around, chicken as hell, and somehow, he will pick up the runs while he is there. But I have always been too naïve and too impatient to play with my average in mind.

'Partly this is a lack of determination, and partly, I admit, a lack of professionalism. I don't have that dogged approach within me: I can hardly ever go out there and block, block, block. I'd be a better cricketer if I did. I'd be a hugely better cricketer in statistical terms, as I would if I bowled better to nine-ten-jack. I give too many runs away when I'm bowling, because I am sometimes trying to do something special that I shouldn't try. I am not plugging away, content to bore my man out.'

Indeed, John Woodcock, *The Times* cricket correspondent, hypothesises that Edmonds' lengthy, and somewhat uncharacteristic string of maidens in India on the 1984–85 tour came about partly because of his problems with his run-up. 'He had lost his rhythm, and so he wasn't able to vary it so much, when he was bowling off one pace. He was forced to ball more conservatively than usual, and so as well as taking all those wickets he did a marvellous job of containment.'

The streak of perversity in Edmonds got in the way of his lifting his Test match batting average against the weakening Australian attack in 1985, and the same streak has cropped up to affect his batting throughout his career. He said: 'I think I would have matured a lot earlier as a cricketer had it not been for Mike Brearley – or had it not been for my reactions to him, at least. Because I should have been a Test match bowler since 1975, an automatic selection. I think, too, that I should have been England captain. But always, there was the problem of Brearley. He didn't rate me as highly as I think he should – and I didn't bowl or bat as well as I should and could have done when I played under him.'

Edmonds retains a great respect for Brearley's abilities as a captain, despite the man's blind spot where Edmonds was concerned. Brearley's gathering of a winning side at Middlesex was a considerable cricketing achievement, he says. 'We have never been a strong batting side. The reason we have done well is because of our top-class bowling. We have got away with our batting limitations, because of the strength of the bowling. We are the other way round to Northamptonshire in this respect, and we are the ones who got the balance right, because we are the side that have picked up the habit of success.' Indeed, it has often seemed in recent years that Middlesex have had a better bowling attack than England, with the West Indian Wayne Daniel, the banned John Emburey and the out-of-favour Phil Edmonds ripping sides apart between them – while England struggled to take a wicket. Middlesex may have often had a long tail, but they have unquestionably had the ability to bowl sides out twice in three-day matches – and that is the way to collect the points that win championships.

126

'Brearley's most important legacy to Middlesex has been attitude, so that when Mike Gatting took over the captaincy from him, he inherited not only a first-class bowling side, but also the attitude that it is a captain's job to attack. He had grown up in the tradition that a captain makes things happen all the time. Had he learned his cricket at a different county, with a more defensive tradition, he might well have turned out to be a completely different sort of captain. But because of the Middlesex tradition that Brearley established, Gatting is a very aggressive captain: that is the way he has learned to see the job.'

Edmonds' reputation for standoffishness can be misleading. He rubs along all right with his team colleagues, and enjoys the send-up and banter that is a part of every cricket dressing-room everywhere. But he still hates to be underestimated. He hit the roof when he went to play Leicestershire in 1985, and arrived to discover that he had been dropped in favour of a fourth seamer. It was not so much being dropped, as going all the way to Grace Road, Leicester to be dropped, that annoyed him. In fact, the incident, though much talked about in the press, had no serious repercussions. Middlesex have a policy of treating their senior players like grown-ups, and Edmonds was on his way back to London as soon as a sprog had arrived to take his place and handle the drinks tray. 'I said a fourth seamer was a waste of time, and I was right. It was certainly a seamer's pitch, but Norman (Cowans) and Wayne (Daniel) took all the wickets, and the fourth seamer hardly did a thing.' The incident prompted an 'Edmonds=Row' kneejerk reaction among the press, but otherwise failed to mar what had been, for Edmonds, a remarkably peaceful as well as successful season.

Edmonds admires the old pro types, and that quite sincerely, but he also has a great deal of respect for inspirational cricketers: the men incapable of putting together a string of average-boosting scores but who will, once in a while, do something extraordinary. 'Roland Butcher wins two matches a year for Middlesex. You must accept that he's never going to be a rock-solid batsman with an average of 40. And you must have him in the side, because he will give you 32 points a year.'

Edmonds is something of the same type of player himself. He is not like one of the brilliantly competent golfing pros who will be able to grind his way to 14th position with a par at every hole.

127

'I should have been a far more effective cricketer throughout the years, but for so many reasons, I remained unfulfilled till very late in the day – and I still haven't fulfilled my full potential. That is one of the things that keeps me in the game – though in some ways I know I will never achieve all I could, and perhaps should have done. I will never captain England now. I lost my chance when I lost the vice-captaincy at Middlesex. It was a pity on my account, and perhaps a pity for England because I would, I think, have been a good and aggressive captain, as well as an imaginative one.'

But Edmonds has resigned himself to being one of the troops. His position in any team has a little tang of uneasiness about it. Steve Archibald, the Spurs and Barcelona footballer, once said: 'Team spirit is an illusion you only glimpse after you have won.' There are ways in which Edmonds can relate to that. Indeed, even after victory, Edmonds does not fit comfortably into a team situation. There is a very strange picture of the England team celebrating their series victory over India in 1984–85. The boys are all grinning like maniacs, chucking the drink over each other, and generally going over the top. Sitting to one side, sipping from his glass, apparently unaffected by the crazed celebrations, is Edmonds, looking thoroughly out of place.

Edmonds is not a team man, in the normally accepted, rah-rah sense of the term. It is not that he plays cricket selfishly, with personal gain first in his priorities and the team nowhere. In his fielding especially, in his encouragement of his colleagues, he is very much a team man, when everyone is out there and the blood flowing hot and strong. In his batting, when it comes off, as well as in the plying of his own specialist trade as a bowler, he cannot be accused of running down the team to pursue his own ends. But somehow, he doesn't belong in crowds, he doesn't adapt to all-lads-together situations. Some colleagues have been bothered by this: they feel that Edmonds is treating them with a measure of contempt. This is not the case: he just lacks the mentality of a joiner-inner. Joining-in is, for many players, one of the great pleasures of team sports. To be all lads together, with victory under the belt and the beer waiting to go the same way, is for such people a holy joy. But here, Edmonds does not find himself affected by the team spirit: and it is at moments like this, more than most, that he wishes he had been a golfer.

CHAPTER 11

BACK IN THE FOLD

By 1984, Phil Edmonds had had enough. He began the season with retirement in his mind, and by June he was determined to give up the game in September. Business beckoned: and it was high time he succeeded at something. His cricket career had been a catalogue of frustrations, and he had come to terms with the fact that it would now end with a whimper. He even accepted the fact that he would never captain Middlesex, and never get back in the England team. Cricket was a saga of lost chances and endless disappointments. There was nothing for it but to retire. There was, quite simply, nothing left to play for. He had had a bellyfull of failure.

By the end of that season, David Gower too, had had enough of failure. He had led his country to a 5–0 home defeat at the hands of the West Indies: the series that will always be remembered as the Blackwash Summer. He said: 'By September I felt like the character in the Spike Milligan poem – the one that goes:

"The boy stood on the burning deck.

Twit." '

'And I think I will find the Blackwash Summer more and more galling as I get older. When the memories have faded a little, the figures will still be absolutely clear. When my playing days are over, I will say: five-nil! How could we possibly have lost all five?'

Despite this disaster, Gower remained the man in charge. For a start, there was no one else. Also, there were extenuating circumstances. England were still without the banned South African 'rebels', and the West Indies of 1984 were perhaps the most fearsome Test side in the history of the game, with four fast bowlers at or near their peaks. Not a team in the world could have stood up to them. It was the truth: it was not much comfort, especially as Gower's next assignment looked almost as tough as facing the West Indies' steam-roller philosophy of cricket. Gower was invited to lead England through a tour of India.

Another series defeat looked very much on the cards. No one had forgotten England's previous tour there, the tour in which India had won the first Test and then closed up the next four, to win 1–0 in what was perhaps the most borinng Test series ever played. Keith Fletcher, the England captain, and Sunil Gavaskar competed as to who could orchestrate the most tedious cricket, until the entire series became a kind of dog-in-the-manger contest.

India is always a hard country to tour. It is the most culture-shocking place on earth: terrifyingly claustrophobic, and it tends to bring out the xenophobic, siege mentality side of many an England cricketer. The cricket itself is full of problems, with mad crowds, intense heat and iffy umpires. Even the West Indies lost a series there in 1978–79. English teams are traditionally troubled in India: they are troubled physically by climate and food; they are troubled mentally by the strangeness of the place. It was not a tour in which Gower could confidently expect to win a reputation as a great captain. The stage looked set for another disaster.

Spin bowling remains a central consideration for any Indian tour, even if the golden age of Indian spin is now over, and with it, the Indian habit of preparing raging turners for their boys. It still made sense for Gower to think in terms of using spin as a strike force, as well as a mere containing device. When it came to the pre-tour selection discussions, Gower had made his mind up – and as a determined captain should, he was determined to carry the meeting.

When I asked Gower who had been instrumental in bringing Edmonds back into the England fold, he held his hand up like a schoolboy admitting, with secret glee, that he was the one who had let the firework off in the playground. 'Guilty!' he said. 'Yes, I was the one who wanted Edmonds back. In fact, it had been a perpetual mystery to me why he had not been in the side for years before. When it came to picking the spinners for the party, I immediately plumped for Edmonds. The other selectors were wary, and asked:

"Yes, but can you handle him?" I told them: "I'll take full responsibility for that." For I had absolutely no trepidation about picking him. I like him, I'm very happy with him.'

In the meantime, Edmonds himself had not been idle. For a start, he had taken 77 first class wickets in the season. Secondly, there are few people in the game as quick as he is at sniffing the wind. Throughout the summer, he had seen England fail all along the line to find anyone capable of bowling at the West Indians. Nick Cook, the slow-left-armer, who had done so well on turning wickets the previous season, and who had given selectors an apparently heaven-sent reason for leaving Edmonds out, bowled in three Tests and took five wickets at an average of 59.4. Only the fading Bob Willis did worse. John Emburey was still banned, so there was the easy spinning option gone. The cupboard looked singularly bare of spin-bowlers when Gower planned his trip to India.

Edmonds could see this quite clearly. 'I spoke to David when Middlesex played Leicestershire, and asked him: "What's the story? How are you picking your guys for the winter?" and David asked me: "Why – are you interested in coming to India?" I said: "Of course I am!"' (It is significant that even Gower thought that Edmonds might not really want to play for England. Edmonds, though he has his eccentric side, is not *that* peculiar.) 'Anyway, David said: "I want to take the best side I can." We left it at that – but I felt encouraged. Then, when I thought he was wavering, I orchestrated a little campaign in the media for my selection. It seemed to me obvious that I should go. I had my column in *The Mail on Sunday*, so I was able to state my case there. I spoke to various journalists I knew, at receptions and so on, and sowed the seed, just letting them know that in my opinion, I was the obvious selection. I was interviewed on Radio 4, and was asked, did I think I would tour? My reply was aimed directly at the selectors: "There is no way they can leave me out this time." When the press boys followed up all this, I was deliberately Muhammed Ali-ish. *The Star* ran a story that said: if Gower is strong enough, Edmonds will go. And I thought, if David reads this, he must pick me. So all in all, I wasn't exactly surprised when I heard that I was going. Just very, very relieved.'

In fact, the selection of the spinners of the party showed a certain amount of boldness and imagination. Vic Marks went as a one-day specialist, and Pat Pocock, a lad of 38, was invited to go for what was certainly going to be his last fling. And it was Edmonds and Pocock between them who levelled the series from one-down. The first Test – which India won in Bombay – was the first time Edmonds had played in a Test match abroad since he had threatened to beat up Mike Brearley when 12th man in Perth. Which was not a total coincidence. Edmonds was not considered to be a bad tourist: he was considered an impossible tourist. But Gower, a man whose captaincy had been the target of much criticism throughout the summer of the Blackwash, decided that he was capable of going one better than Brearley, the great guru of captaincy: he decided that he could 'handle' Edmonds.

Vic Marks wrote, in his diary of the tour: 'Henri was most impressive, and is the most intriguing character on the tour. At times remote and aloof, at others helpful and perceptive, and always aggressive on the field. The social committee has already fined him for not being the trouble-maker he's alleged to be, as he has been conspicuously co-operative with the management, and has earned the gratitude of everyone by procuring some high-quality Scotch from Johnnie Walker.' Paul Downton has been quoted earlier in these pages in praise of the way in which Edmonds comfortably assumed the mantle of number one bowler on the tour: in truth, he expanded like a flower in the sun under the warmth of his own success, his own acceptance – for the first time – as a top England man.

The turning point of the tour came on the last day of the second Test, in Delhi: the day England came back from one down to level the series. Tim Robinson had made things possible with his splendid 160 (for which members of the party wrote the song 'Old Man Robbo', who 'just keeps batting along'). India needed an impressive score in the second innings, and, under relentless pressure from Pocock and Edmonds, they failed to achieve it. Wickets fell as the pressure increased: the more the wickets fell, the more the pressure, and the spinners both bowled as men inspired. Even a succession of rejected, heart-rending appeals did not daunt them: India were dismissed, leaving England two hours to make 125, and, with a scare and a scamper, they made it for the loss of a couple of wickets. The second innings bowling figures from the two England spinners are the most remarkable aspect of the match. Pocock had

38.4-9-93-4, and Edmonds 44-24-60-4: not bad for a bowler who is meant to be unable to settle back and bowl a string of maidens.

England also won the fourth Test to finish the series 2–1 up: this time it was Neil Foster who got the wickets, and Graeme Fowler and Mike Gatting the runs. Edmonds and Foster, with 14 each, were the top wicket-takers of the series, and Edmonds was the top wicket-taker on the tour, with 32. Edmonds was also, by a long way, the most active bowler. In Tests he bowled 276.1 overs, with 104 maidens, and in all matches he bowled 498.1 overs with 184 maidens. Edmonds had what was, in every way, a remarkable tour.

The following summer showed early signs of being a memorable one. It was, after all, an Ashes summer, and everything pointed to a close series: a young and promising Australian side against an England team that was beginning to find its feet. As he arrived, the Australian captain Allan Border said: 'Any one who misses this series is crazy. Because it's going to be a beauty.' He was right. Though perhaps he would prefer to forget it himself. But it would be a great mistake to undervalue England's achievement in winning it 3–1: true, the Australian side went from disaster to disaster after they had returned home. But that was because the young side had been totally demoralised by England's successful battle for the upper hand in the Ashes series – so much so that they have struggled ever since. The two sides were considered absolutely even stevens until the fifth Test – a Test Australia narrowly failed to save, and which they lost thanks to a freak dismissal brought about by Edmonds. That failure affected Australia, and the innings defeat in the final Test pulled them apart. Australia went home like men sand-bagged.

But England celebrated Edmonds' triumphant tour of India by leaving him out of the first Test match against Australia. That provoked the archetypal Edmonds response when the press asked for his comment: 'They must be mad!' Mad or not, England won the match – it was at the traditional seamers' paradise of Headingley. Another massive innings from Robinson set things in motion, and Botham and Emburey were the best bowlers. Edmonds came back for the second Test, which Australia won despite Edmonds' impressive performance on the final day.

It was the day in which Border and Edmonds began their duel that was to last for the rest of the series. Border was by far the best

133

batsman Australia had, and so naturally Edmonds couldn't wait to bowl at him. Their determination to do each other down was immense: each admired the other greatly, and each was determined to stuff the other out of sight.

'It was a very friendly Test series,' Edmonds said. 'Even though I deliberately tried to hit Border when he was fielding at short leg. Holland, their little leggie, was bowling some innocuous stuff, and I went to whack him for four. But I accidentally hit Border on the shin, really hard. So I went up to him, and said: "Sorry about that, hope you're OK." He was in real pain, and he turned around and snapped at me: "Shut-up and get on with your batting!" So I said: "if that's the way you feel, I hope it's broken!" And I went berserk. Often my batting, as well as my bowling, gets better when I'm annoyed. I tried to larrup the ball and hit old Border again. I tried so hard that I got myself caught out at slip. I was still annoyed with him when I got to bowl at him though – and because of that, I bowled really well. Funnily enough, in that innings, he happened to hit me when I was fielding close. It was an accident, I know. He said nothing, and I said nothing. And we laughed about it later: he told me: "I was waiting for you to tell me to shut up and get on with my batting."

'I think my bowling to Border was one of the crucial parts of our win in the series. He did incredibly well, but never with complete freedom. And when he tried to slog me out of the attack – which wasn't a stupid tactic – it didn't come off.' Matthew Engel wrote in *The Guardian* that Border's 'form may have given him illusions of immortality'. At any rate, at Old Trafford he charged Edmonds like a crazy man and got himself stumped – the first stumping by an England wicket-keeper in a home Test for five years, incidentally. Edmonds said: "If he had got away with it, he would have considered me a poor bowler, and would have felt psychologically one-up on me for the rest of the series and beyond. That is the way so many confrontations in cricket work. Take Zaheer Abbas: I bowled him with an arm ball when I was at Cambridge, in 1972, and it was a beautiful ball. Ever since then, I have been one-up on him – and he is one of the finest batsmen in the game. He really rates me because of that one delivery, and forever after was extra careful against me. And I sensed that, so I bowled even better at him.

'With Allan Border, I knew he was ready to attack me; even so early in his innings, I could sense that he was going to come down the track at me. So I bowled extra slowly, and he was too hot-headed to adjust, and the ball was through him. It was a pretty ordinary ball in fact, but it was one that maintained my slight edge over Border.'

Edmonds was a vital part of the team throughout that splendid Ashes summer. His bowling at top-line batsmen was crucial, and his tigerish close-in fielding was a terrific bonus. He held seven catches in the series, and also took the finest catch of the summer – at third man of all places – a memorable running, leaping and rolling tour de force. It was not only Botham, the bowler, who was peeved that the delivery was declared a no-ball. In the series as a whole, the seamers had the biggest share of the wickets, and Emburey, who played one Test match more, beat Edmonds' haul by a few wickets. But Edmonds, with 15 strikes, most of them important ones, was a central part of the Australia-crushing operation: indeed, it was off his bowling that the decisive wicket was taken. Australia, with Phillips and Ritchie at the wicket, were in the process of saving the fifth Test with some panache, and looked in little trouble. Phillips then tried to crash Edmonds through the offside. Indeed, thoughout the series, Phillips tried to crash everyone through the offside, so much so that Botham on occasions set four gulleys to him. But this time, the ball failed to go for four: it bounced high off Allan Lamb's instep and ballooned up for Gower to take the catch. A freak dismissal, now generally agreed to be a wholly fair one, but one that caused the Australian morale to crumble. They lost that, and the next Test by an innings. And it was England's series.

'One of the nice things about the series,' Gower said, 'was that when I made a bowling change, it really was a bowling change. Not just a change of bowler's name. I had Botham to do his pace and fire bit, Taylor to bowl moderate swing, Ellison to bowl enormous swing, and Edmonds and Emburey as completely contrasting spinners. It was the spinners that put me in control for long periods of the series – and that meant that I could use Both in bursts, as a strike bowler, and not a stock bowler. I didn't have to rely on Both all the time – which made him all the more effective.' In short, Gower had a team of bowlers he could trust. No one had to be molly-coddled. And indeed, Gower's decision to trust Edmonds as a team-mate was part of his success in two successive series.

'He should have been in the team years ago,' Gower insisted. 'He has suffered from his own temperament, and when things do not go his own way, he does let it go a bit. He has not always been very good at dealing with captains, particularly Mike Brearley. People tend to be wary of him, because he is a professional wind-up artist, who loves debate for its own sake. But he has done me no disservice, and I have enjoyed him very much.'

Brearley was a captain who liked to impress his personality on every possible facet of the game. And of course, he could not get on with Edmonds. But Gower's captaincy is very different. He can get along with practically everybody, and certainly with the perennially 'difficult' Phil Edmonds. This is because Gower – with his own personal cliché of 'laid-back' – is not about to insist on his own best-laid schemes at every turn. He likes to leave well alone, and as such, has shown himself a fine, low-profile captain of a winning team. It is not his nature to mould men to his liking: he is the sort to adapt himself to the most effective winning combination of players. To pick a quarrel with Gower would be like picking a fight with a ghost: there is nothing to hold on to. Gower has not been over-praised for his captaincy – perhaps critics are too much used to successful captains being men in the Brearley mould – but Gower's policy of quietly accepting men for their abilities has been, in pre-vious series, an unquestionable success. He has won from one-down in India: he has won the Ashes back. You can't argue with that.

'You must expect a man like Edmonds to assert his individuality every now and then,' Gower said. 'Every match will be character-ised by the odd Henri-ism. A wise captain will accept that as part of the man. Every now and then, he will lose a little balance and control, but if you want to use his talents, you must let that go.' Here Gower demonstrates a wisdom that, in this particular case, Brearley was never able to show. 'Edmonds thinks more deeply about the game than most,' Gower continued. 'Especially when it comes to getting a batsman out. I don't always think that batsmen are as intelligent as Henri appears to think. But he remains a man that will do you a good job.

'He enjoys himself on the field, which is great. Even when he gets angry, or otherwise temperamental, it is normally because he is angry with himself. He has such high standards for himself, and great pride in his ability to bowl. He hates it when he slips up, and he loves it when he can out-think the batter – and as a matter of fact, he also loves to out-think his captain. He is always particular about his field placings, and here again, most of the time I am happy to go along with him. If he wants to take a certain risk, that's normally absolutely fine with me.

'He did well in every way when we were in India. There was a running gag throughout the tour that he was a trouble-maker – because he took such pains not to be one. Of course, he is a loner, with his headphones and his books, but so long as his contribution is fine – in team meetings and on the pitch – then I am happy. He likes to make his point in team meetings, in fact, and sometimes gets shouted down as well – but he accepts that as part of the fun.'

Gower has two other traits that make him a marvellous captain for Edmonds. He gives him a lot of overs, and he doesn't tell him how to bowl them. Gower is a quick left-arm batter, not a slow left-arm bowler: 'Henri has been bowling slow left-arm for 15 years now, so I am hardly likely to out-think him in that area. So long as I know about half of what he is trying to do, I am content. I will guide less experienced bowlers a good deal, especially over field-placings. But 95 per cent of the time, when Henri is bowling I will go along with what he wants.' In short, Gower treats Edmonds as Edmonds would most like to be treated. He gives him the ball often and wants him to try and get top-line batsmen out. In the Ashes series, most of the time when Gower changed from seam to spin, he threw the ball first to Edmonds – to bowl aggressively at the cream of the opposition. Just what Edmonds likes – and does – best. The scent of Chanel No 5 no longer gets up Edmonds' nose.

Gower also appreciates Edmonds' low boredom threshold, along with the theatricality of his nature and his love of being involved. Some people have found these attributes tiresome: not Gower, however, who thoroughly appreciates the phenomenal catches Edmonds took around the bat throughout the summer. 'His catch off the no-ball at third man was the best of the season,' Gower said. 'And it showed the versatility of the man.'

Edmonds has been criticised for his hand-clapping encourage-ment of the fielding side when his blood is up. Bob Taylor, of all people, has expressed his stern displeasure at this. ('I kept looking over to him, wondering if he was feeling all right.') Gower, however, thinks Edmonds' histrionics are a real bonus.

Before Gower and Edmonds had brought about Edmonds' rehabilitation, Edmonds had acquired the reputation of being a uniquely dreadful sort of person. Newcomers to the England side were mystified to find, instead of the authority-flouting monster, a man of charm and humour. Edmonds and Robinson got on particularly well, despite Robinson's having to share a room with him in India, and put up with all the attendant horrors of the World Service at four in the morning. 'I love his sense of humour,' Robinson said. 'The way he never smiles when he is making jokes. That is a habit of his which confuses people, and helped them to misunderstand him. He and I have built up this thing when we always shake hands after a Test match, and say, very solemnly: "A great privilege to have played with you." And the other person replies, without smiling: "A great privilege to have played with *you*."'

Against all the predictions of those who had learned the story of Edmonds the perpetual misfit, he became a central part of a successful team, captained by an understanding man, and playing alongside a bunch of players with whom the liking and the respect is mutual. It is, in a way, almost too good to be true: after 14 years of varying degrees of frustration, Edmonds became a central part in the most successful England team for some time, with those two successive series wins. Edmonds believes that he should have played in 100 Test matches. But his part in 10 Tests in two successive series has brought him more glory than many an international cricketer has tasted. Late in the day, Edmonds was given a chance to make up for his past frustrations: he has seized his chances with a miser's glee: and English cricket has been the richer because of it.

CHAPTER 12

WORLDLY WISE

When sportsmen fill out those silly questionnaires, as mentioned before in these pages, the answers are, of course, always the same. Favourite film stars: Clint Eastwood/Jane Fonda. Favourite television programme: Fawlty Towers. Television programme you always switch off: party political broadcasts and current affairs programmes, etc.

Phil Edmonds, typically, does not fit into that sort of categorisation. He loves party political broadcasts and he is fascinated by the media.

'All establishments are surely the same, in that their principle function is to perpetuate themselves. In order to do this, they must condition the way people think. In this country, we pride ourselves on being a reasonably democratic society – but how democratic are we, I wonder? Sure, you can stand up in Hyde Park and say anything you want without any obvious penalty. But if you have the effrontery to propound a message that looks *dangerous* to the powers that be, then retribution is likely to be swift. Look at Philip Agee, a man who said in the mid-70s that all international phone calls are tapped. Of course, he was 10 years too early with this. He could have excited an outcry about the infringement of liberty – and so it was necessary to discredit him. Now, after 10 years of conditioning, we accept that all phone calls are tappable, and the most common attitude is "so what? What have we got to hide?" And we accept that the National Security Agency in America has the technical capability to beam into any phone call anywhere in America.

'Coming from Zambia in the mid-60s gave us all an insight into the way people are manipulated. By the early 1960s, the policy of taking a European, as opposed to a colonial standpoint on all economic questions had been established. The only problem was to convince the people that this was right. This eventually ended with the sham of the referendum. And so anybody who opposed Europe had to be discredited. There were two people at opposite ends of the political spectrums who had strong reservations about the issue: Enoch Powell and Tony Benn. These two were labelled as extremists, and identified with the "no" vote. At the same time, the whole weight of the so-called independent media was behind a "yes" vote – this even included that most propaganda orientated programme, *The Archers*, with good old Phil Archer the pillar of the Establishment, saying that going into Europe was undoubtedly a Good Thing. And when the time came, 16 million people duly made their mark in the "yes" column.'

Edmonds' interest in the exploitation of the media goes beyond the frank vote-catching of the party political broadcasts. He sees the media as the arm, not so much of individual politicians and their parties, as of the Establishment: the great faceless machine that keeps any society under a loose, but decisive degree of control.

'The Soviet establishment does this through direct propaganda. The British establishment controls what people think in a more subtle way, but control is what they are striving for. There is a difference between Radio Moscow broadcasts – which I listen to a lot – and *The Archers*. But both are methods by which the Establishment controls the people's thoughts.

'A further way the Establishment seeks control is through information gathering. This can be done by such indirect means as the tapping of international telephone calls, or through such things as Thomson's Local Directory and little Neighbourhood Watch schemes. Thomson's directories have a friendly, neighbourly look to them – but in fact Thomson's is an international organisation, and this is a major exercise in the gathering of information. Neighbourhood Watch is basically a scheme for householders to protect themselves from burglars by reporting suspicious-looking strangers in their street. But it is a very small step from reporting strangers to reporting on your mates. And I was brought up at a time when our neighbours, some of them, were reporting on us, because we were an anti-Establishment family.'

Edmonds, as I have said, is a complete information junkie. He requires enormous fixes of facts on everything, cannot bear to switch a television or a radio off, and buys newspapers and magazines by the bushel. He doesn't necessarily believe all the information he receives, but his doubts make it all the more fascinating. 'You must accept that the media are going to put a slant onto their reporting of all major events, no matter how independent they claim to be. Let us go back to the miners' strike. The notion we got was this: the miners are thugs, and Scargill is a dangerous fanatic. This did not come through by deliberate unsubtle propaganda. It is the much subtler, much more insidious method of selection. Police attacks on the miners were never shown: but in colour, in our living-rooms, every night, we saw miners attacking policemen.

'In a similar way, newspapers operate a kind of pseudo-balance. They are reasonably objective if you read the entire story, or at least, they can claim to be. But in truth the headline, and the order in which the facts appear, gives the entire story an implicit slant.'

Edmonds likes the phrase 'the conspiracy theory' to describe this effect, but he is not talking about a deliberate, thought-out conspiracy. He is talking about the implicit conspiracy that is born of the common interest of men in power: their common aim being simply to remain in power. 'People were shocked when they heard that men who work for the BBC are screened by MI5. I would be shocked if they were not. Everyone, in any important position, in the media and elsewhere, goes through a kind of screening process. That is to say, if they are not the right kind of chap, their employers won't give them the job. You wouldn't give a talented journalist a job as editor of the BBC News if he happened to be a committed Marxist: he would be considered the wrong sort of chap.

'This is an extension of the old public school syndrome: the old notion that you had to go to the right school if you wanted the right job. In some areas this still applies literally: but almost anywhere, it happens in a subtler way: you don't get the job if you're the wrong sort of guy. This committed Marxist wouldn't get the job as script editor of *The Archers*, because it would be against all the traditions of the programme. And on *The Archers*, all kinds of topical issues are discussed. Who is it that always comes up with the establishment view? The most respected, decent, upright character on the show – Philip Archer himself.'

Edmonds revels in the incongruity of this particular argument. He will not go so far as to claim that there is a person there who ensures that *The Archers* conforms to certain political notions. But it happens that the character of Philip Archer demands that he put himself forward as the voice of reason. And he is, unquestionably, an Establishment man.

For Edmonds, the Establishment is not a matter of political parties. He does not see the Establishment as specifically right wing: he sees it as a supporter of the political neuter: the great don't-rock-the-boat philosophy of the unseen men who work behind the politicians: in particular the faceless, un-elected rulers of the nation: the civil service. 'It is the "Yes, Minister" syndrome. The programme makes comic capital out of a situation that is real enough: the dominant influence of the invisible men of the civil service. It is my belief that what the Establishment, as typified by the civil service, want more than anything is not a strong right wing majority, but a hung parliament that works on tiny, oscillating majorities, one which allows the influence of the civil service to grow unchecked.

'And it is my opinion that television and radio reflect this view with a tacit support of the Alliance parties and the policy of proportional representation. Television forms the Celluloid Centre of British politics.'

Edmonds may be a man of boundless political cynicism, but he is not, he says, opposed to the Establishment, or what he sees as its manipulations. 'I'm an Establishment man myself,' he said. 'Establishments need to establish stability in order to work. That is why you do not take wild experiments, you appoint the guy with the old school tie, because you know exactly what he will do, what he will believe, and why. I don't object to that – I am just fascinated by the way in which things happen and the way in which the way people think – and therefore what they do – is controlled.'

His incessant reading, listening and watching habits give him plenty of points of comparison. He sees BBC presenters like Sir Robin Day as propagandists for the Establishment and as such, not greatly different to the voice of Radio Moscow. And this is why he is baffled by the frequent cutbacks made in the BBC World Service. 'On altruistic grounds, the World Service should continue to give as large a service as possible, because it is a fine service, and one which gives people all over the world important facts and insights. And from a realistic point of view, it makes for a vast increase in British influence and, indeed, in worldwide affection for the British. On purely pragmatic grounds it is a wonderful way of increasing British influence at very low cost. In the same way, Britain no longer gives the same number of scholarships and things like cadetships at places like Sandhurst, to pupils from developing countries, another important way of increasing affection and for the country and the country's influence. Instead, the guys probably now go to Beijing.'

As a former colonial, he is fascinated by British attitude to its remaining colonial interest. 'Billions were spent on the Falklands War – so that people who want to be British can stay British, we were told. What, then, about the people in Northern Ireland, who want to remain British, but who face the increasingly likely prospect of a United Ireland? It is the same situation as the Falklanders faced – unwanted absorption by a different country – yet because of the way the media presents the problem, we are conditioned not to think of the question in the same way. The Establishment must beware of the gut feeling of the man in the street and the potential charge of treachery.

'I have travelled a lot, thanks to cricket, and having a glimpse of so many countries maintains your interests in these countries afterwards. All that gives a breadth to your world view. Because of that, as well as my African upbringing, I do not see things from the traditional, insular, British viewpoint. And I can understand why some acts, that might look completely irrational, from a foreign country, are completely inevitable.

'But Britain is the place where I live, and I wouldn't want to live anywhere else. This is the society I want to live in. I am fascinated by the way all societies work, and the way in which the media controls so much. I think people should realise how their society does work. But I don't want to change the society itself at all.'

When Edmonds talks politics – a not infrequent occurrence – and expounds his own notions of political realism, he comes over as a man stuffed with worldly wisdom. Not all his own personal dealings have been characterised by the same calm understanding of what is expedient. 'He may talk about the conspiracy theory – but I wish to God he was a better conspirator himself,' Frances said. Many of his personal dealings have been characterised not by shrewdness, but by its antithesis: a reckless naïvete: a vague belief that if such a notion is good sense, people cannot fail to go along with it.

This naïvete in personal dealings manifested itself most clearly in the long and problematic relationship with Mike Brearley. 'I see now that I should have made efforts to be nice, sensible and rational and to get along with him, to establish a harmonious working relationship. When he asked me to slog for bonus points after he had batted 70 overs for 70 runs, I should have said: "Certainly, Brears", instead of getting uptight, and asking him "is this a team game or what?" Stupid, naïve way to behave: and I could not believe things wouldn't work out, that my own abilities as a bowler would force things to improve. Perhaps they worked out in the end, but I wasted years because of my naïve approach to my relationship with Brears. In my own career, I showed none of the canniness I can see so clearly in many shrewd professional cricketers. In personal relationships in cricket, I have shown a lack of tact and sense that is amazing from someone who is supposed to be reasonably intelligent. I have been personally naïve too many times in the past, and it is that quality that has caused me trouble throughout my cricket career. I suppose it goes back to my Zambian upbringing: I was used to settling disputes with the gloves on – and then forgetting all about it. Not everyone sees things as simply. If I had been a worldly wise cricketer, I would have saved myself years of frustration.'

CHAPTER 13

THE LAST GREAT AMATEUR

Edmonds would not argue with those who think his torso is worth a second look. But surely this was going too far. As he sat in his new bathing drawers by the side of the Hilton's swimming pool (a keskadee calling from the top of a coconut tree) the world's interest in his torso was becoming obsessive. Second looks were simply not enough. Strangers kept approaching him and begging for a closer inspection. 'You should have seen it before,' Edmonds said vaingloriously. His torso was so spectacular that it was photographed and printed on the back page of the *Today* newspaper as the publication sought to win readers in its first week of publication. Never mind Samantha Fox: Today had Edmonds – in colour!

Why not, indeed? The colour of the torso was nothing less than spectacular. The Hilton was in Port of Spain, Trinidad, and Edmonds was bearing two enormous and hideous bruises after being struck twice by the fastest bowler in the world. Had it not been for a new cricket invention he would, he said, have been killed. The old, uncomfortable pad, that had to be Elastoplasted across the chest, has been superseded by a lightweight vest with pockets of protective foam. The makers, Air-O-Wear, developed the garment after their success with a spinal protector for jockeys. Edmonds is rightly grateful for it: he was struck over the heart by a beamer from Patrick Patterson. 'Without that vest, my ribs would have snapped like twigs,' he said, not wholly without relish. The bruises had by then faded from deep black to mere iridescent purple. Below the beamer's bruise was a second: Patterson followed with a rib ball that found its target. One hell of a game, cricket.

'I'm enjoying this tour immensely,' Edmonds was telling me when he wasn't answering enquiries about his torso. 'I find batting against the West Indies tremendous fun.' In the first Test match in the series, which was played on a snake-pit of a wicket at Sabina Park, Jamaica, Edmonds had the rare distinction of being out twice in the same innings. Patterson's beamer sent him staggering into his wicket, and this at once prompted a huge appeal from the West Indian fielders. But the umpire ruled out the dismissal, on the grounds that the beamer was an unfair delivery. The Laws are clear on the point. Edmonds fought on a while longer, but England still lost by ten wickets in three days, and took a pasting that cast a shadow over the rest of the tour.

By the time the team had moved on to Trinidad, corporate resolve was cracking and crumbling. The two weeks they spent on the island were an unmitigated disaster. True, there was a splendid, sumptuous win in the one day international there, but all hopes that this success – on a much flatter wicket than Jamaica – could be followed up in the Test match were quickly thrown out of the window. England had lost the game by tea on the first day, when once again the batting was flattened by the West Indian steam-roller method of playing cricket. And after that, there was no room for anything else but an extremely gallant rearguard action, highlighted by a day of quite splendid spin bowling from Edmonds and Emburey. Had they had a total worth bowling at, England might have thought about saving the match, or better. But a first innings total of 176 gave the side no leeway: and furthermore, the mood of depression was already cast.

To come from England and to watch an England side collapsing about one's ear was a strange experience, and, in a macabre way, fascinating. People care so much about the progress of England's cricket team: for most of us, a Test match is a splendid step outside the mundane. But for most Test cricketers, Test cricket *is* the mundane. And with that goes a kind of workday acceptance of defeat that I found immensely disconcerting. I must add that Edmonds, true to his stance as the last great amateur, was wholly untouched by this. The West Indies needed a mere 92 in their second innings to win. Edmonds said: 'I went out believing that we could bowl them out for 90. And we could have done.' In the event, the West Indies got them for three wickets, though the spinners did make them work for the runs. If only, if only there had been a decent total to bowl at . . . it was a deeply frustrating match for the spinners.

The match, and indeed, the entire series had Edmonds seething with frustration. The combination of the dour, workaday 'professional' approach to the game, coupled with the giddy amateur thinking in the way any tour is run, had him shaking his head in disbelief. 'Can you believe that before we played our first match in the West Indies we hardly had any proper practice save for a few days in Barbados and before the first Test we had only three matches on wickets totally unrepresentative of the Test wickets? Cricket is a pretty lethal game these days – and we hardly practised or had the appropriate facilities for practice! Can you imagine McEnroe not bothering to practise before Wimbledon? Can you imagine Ballesteros saying, ah well, never mind, it's only The Open, I'll just smack a couple of balls on the driving range and then get started? Steve Davis practises for four hours every day he is not playing a tournament. And Eric Bristow, the darts champion, he will throw darts all day to get into good nick for a competition. But the England cricket team – who were due to play the best side in the world in a series in which people could be hurt and ran the risk of being killed (and notwithstanding the bad weather) – we seemed to be just Making Do. I could not believe it.'

When England first went to the West Indies in 1930, they were missionaries for the game. Now they go as underdogs to the world champions, and are part of multi-buck industry. Yet they still practise on grounds like the Cow Patch and the Goat Field: these names are not merely picturesque. Remember that a West Indies tour starts late. The players go into it after four months away from cricket. It is not just the light they need to get used to. They need time and practice to get their entire games back into shape. Prolonged practice in the West Indies is not a luxury, it is a necessity. The more so since the players on this tour faced the fastest bowlers in the world.

Edmonds said: 'Well, we went to the police ground for our first practice in Antigua, and inevitably, the first rain they'd had for three months fell, so we had no practice in the morning. We went back in the afternoon, and we were able to do a little practice out in the middle. The only problem was that there was no net. That meant we spent most of the afternoon looking for balls in the bush. It was totally ridiculous. So the next day, we were promised that we would be able to have an extensive practice, that there would be a net, and a perfect wicket right from the start. The groundsman decided to water the pitch that evening, and to roll it evening and morning ready for the start. Fine. But the problem here was that he had no covers. It rained a bit in the night . . . and then a herd of cows walked all over the wicket. All over the pitch there were hoof-prints an inch deep. So now the groundsman had to re-water the pitch and then re-roll it, to get rid of all the prints. So no practice in the morning; finally managed to get some in the afternoon. Next morning we were out there in a match facing men who bowl at the speed of light, including George Ferris, the guy who nearly killed Roland Butcher when he hit him in the face.'

Edmonds was not being xenophobic here, and resenting the poverty of the host nation and wishing that Antigua was a bit more like NW8. It is the entire game of cricket's lack of organisation that exasperates him. There is a great deal of money in cricket these days: to spend some of it on providing proper practice facilities around Test match grounds all over the world would make sense to the players of every country. What would make better sense still would be for a member of the touring party to travel ahead of the team and make sure that such things as nets, useable wickets and alternative practice grounds are available for the team when it arrives. This represents a professional habit of thought of the kind that would occur to any businessman: you would not dream of going into a key meeting without doing your homework. You get a leg-man to do all the boring, meticulous bits. As a matter of routine, you give yourself the best possible chance of success. 'But no, not in cricket,' Edmonds said. 'Cricket still seems to be obsessed by Making Do.'

Professional sportsmen tend to wrap a great mystique about themselves. They like to make it quite clear that they are different to the rest of us, that they have a different, a 'professional' attitude to their particular sport. 'We're just professional cricketers earning a living,' was the war-cry of Graham Gooch as he led his rebel team in South Africa. 'We've just got to go out there and do a professional job,' is the sort of thing David Gower is always saying. But despite all this, a bumbling amateurism lives on in the professional game. Sometimes it seems that dour 'professionalism' takes over every where the amateur spirit is most appropriate, and that footling amateurism is the attitude when genuine professionalism is what is most needed. Attitudes to practice and preparation seem to be almost dilatory: it seems sometimes that the 'professionalism' is a mere sham: that cricketers are amateurs to their souls, for all that they happen to get paid for playing. Despite the cash, they are content to muddle and Make Do.

Edmonds was annoyed by the way England so easily fell into a losing position in that second Test in Trinidad. We talked about this at length on the rest day, as I sipped Johnnie Walker and Edmonds, playing the next day, stuck to fizzy pop. 'What do you think happens in team meetings?' he challenged. I said that I imagined these were pretty intense occasions: that tactics were discussed at a bafflingly complex level out of the reach of outsiders, and that an upbeat, bullish mood was carefully fostered. Not a bit of it. Frances' joke about 'rah rah' meetings is a jibe at the mood of frustration, depression and even defeatism that the team meeting appeared to be sponsoring. There seems to be an increasing gap between the senior professionals (who had heard it all before and wanted to skim as fast as possible over the cricket talk and then, perhaps, discuss what they did on their days off) and the younger players, eager for advice . . . Advice they sometimes had to battle to obtain from the battle-hardened stars who wanted a beer. It would have been interesting to know what kind of support a test debutant like Greg Thomas received at the team meeting before his first appearance for England. Hopefully, he would have felt able to ask about line and length and just as hopefully, he wouldn't have been fobbed off with the old line, 'Ah, shut up, just get out there and bowl.' Edmonds, after a team meeting, a gathering that is hedged around with the kind of official secrecy that reminds you of the briefing that 'M' used to give James Bond, is not allowed to talk about what goes on. His TCCB contract is also a kind of 'official secrets act', but when these epic secret sessions are over, Edmonds does not act like a man

149

who has emerged from a satisfying and stimulating business conference.

'This is not to say that there is no intelligent and useful discussion of cricket going on. It often happens outside team meetings. For instance, Paul Downton, Embers and I had a long and interesting talk about bowling at the West Indies the other day. It was very helpful to us all. That sort of thing happens all the time, in small groups. But if you are a new boy, maybe you are not getting that kind of informal help. Maybe you are not on those terms with the people who can give you the best sort of help. So I think this sort of thing needs to be organised properly, for everyone's benefit.

'Team meetings tend to be a reflection of the captain. As you might expect, Brears' team meetings were always very formal, and pretty useful.' One wonders, as an observer, if Gower is really a team meeting man. Perhaps, even, he lacks the confidence to talk of canny tactics to this room full of old pros: the thing about Gower is that his is such a sumptuous natural talent that he has never had the need to think deeply about how he does it. Such a thing would probably be counter-productive. But that doesn't help those less richly endowed, those who need to resort to guile and tricks – 99 per cent of all cricketers, in short. In the same way, Gower is not a rabble-rousing sort of chap, and any 'up and-at-'em' talk is liable to ring false. It is a hard job, being a touring captain. You have immense responsibilities on the field at home or away, but on tour every aspect of events comes back to you and reflects you. You carry a huge weight – especially when things start to go wrong.

'I think the captain is under too much pressure', Edmonds said. 'A lot of the pressure could be taken off him if we appointed a team manager – a supremo.'

'You?' I asked.

The length of the pause here was unexpected. I asked the question knowing that Edmonds does not see his future in cricket. But on the other hand, this was an interesting thought: 'Yeeeeeeah. Yes, I could see myself as supremo very easily. If I could devote five years of my life to the job, and didn't get involved in any outside business whatsoever, and took a totally non-amateur approach to the job, it would be fascinating. It would be a crucial decision to have to make. But it would be a wonderfully challenging job for five years.'

Let me emphasise that this was what Americans call a 'blue skies' session, a meeting in which wild speculations and unlikely notions can be discussed without reference to their practicability. Edmonds is sure that if the TCCB were to defy tradition and appoint an England supremo, it has always been assumed that the number one contender would be Bob Willis. However, after the criticism he took ('too close to the senior players') from his part in the tour, his star is perhaps on the wane.

There are a number of things that Edmonds is itching to see achieved, and which the right supremo would be able to implement. In general terms, this is the imposition of genuine professional attitudes, as opposed to the half-baked professionalism on which cricketers pride themselves. Specifics include making use of everything that could help a cricketer to give himself the best possible chance of succeeding. 'Video is one of the most helpful devices for a sportsman,' he said. 'But we don't use it. It would be so useful to be able to watch videos of all the West Indians' recent internationals, and to see for ourselves who was doing what well, who was getting out in what sort of way, and who was having a hard time against whom. It would also be useful to have videos of the matches we play on this tour, to see where we were slipping up, or how our opponents were batting and bowling against us. We should be travelling with a library of video tapes. For example, when I lost my run-up in India, it would have been invaluable had I been able to watch myself bowling with my normal approach. I would have been able re-find my rhythm so much more easily.

'It would not be expensive, nor desperately complicated, to set up such a system. It just needs some one to do it. But I remember when we tried to use video for coaching at Middlesex: I was the only one who would operate it. I ended up with hours and hours of Mike Brearley batting – and not a second of me bowling.'

Using videos, and any other device that would help cricketers, is one aspect of the way a supremo's genuinely professional thinking could operate. The supremo himself would be something of a shatteringly modern device. Edmonds sees the job as total responsibility for team selection, to be in charge of overseeing physical, technical and psychological preparation of the players, as well as assisting the captain with tactical advice. The obvious clash between a captain's and a supremo's areas of responsibility would need to be worked out from the start, but broadly, a supremo would be in charge of strategy and a captain in charge of tactics. 'It would be inevitable that as a supremo, you'd want to step in and discuss tactics between sessions,' Edmonds said.

'Discuss or dictate?' I asked.

'There'd be a temptation to dictate,' Edmonds said. 'So you'd need a strong captain. There would be problems in that area, but I don't suppose they are insuperable.'

Edmonds' supremo would be solely in charge of selection, but would consult heavily. The first people he would turn to would be the first class umpires. After all, these men not only draw their play by being the most astute observers of the game, but they have the best view of it by a hundred yards and more. Furthermore, they concentrate on every ball in every match. 'I'd like to see the umpires in a semi-official position, as aids to selection,' Edmonds said. 'They see all the psychological battles: who comes out on top, who cracks under pressure. When Viv Richards is smashing it all over the park, they know who remains aggressive, and who doesn't want to bowl. Undoubtedly selectors do talk to umpires, in an informal, over-the-bar kind of way. But it would be more helpful still if this were formalised.'

But as Edmonds and I were discussing hypotheses for the game's future, English cricket was in the throes of retreating into its immediate past. The successive series wins over India and Australia had been set aside, and the ghost of the Blackwash summer of 1984 was walking again, as England slid to ignominious defeat in the second Test. It had been hoped that Port of Spain would be the place where England struck back, but it did not work out quite like that. The traumatic battering at Sabina Park had gone too deep.

The political troubles of Trinidad further reduced team morale. Every tour these days is attended by a major political problem of one kind or another, but this time it was directly connected with the cricketers themselves. Guyana had simply refused to allow any England side containing any South African rebel into the country, but Trinidad took a more dodgey course. The cricketers were allowed in, on, as it were, the condition that they had a bad time. The prime minister, George Chambers, had announced that he intended to boycott the cricket. No doubt this was a political stunt: it was, after all, election year in Trinidad.

Furthermore, many other Trinidadians were in favour of a mass boycott of the cricket, and encouraged it with a succession of noisy demonstrations against the touring team. 'Racists go home,' they shouted at the team. Banners proclaimed: 'They hate black people', 'West Indies Cricket Board of Control run by Thatcher', and, rather charmingly, 'Dey fell all ah we born in silly mid on'. Despite this playfulness, the atmosphere was hostile to the English team, who were thoroughly upset by it all.

The security for the team was stepped up hugely as a result of all this. There was an armed guard in the team corridor. Around the Hilton's swimming pool, there were often a couple of policemen, wearing revolvers round their necks on lanyards, and with alsatians on their wrists. And there always seemed to be police in the Hilton car park. If the aim was to increase the siege mentality of the England players, Trinidad accomplished it quite effortlessly.

The cricketers were advised not to leave the hotel alone. The Port of Spain Hilton is a place where it would be nice to spend a weekend, especially if one could leave early on Sunday. The England team were cooped up in there for two weeks because of the hostile environment, leaving only to face the most hostile bowling in the world. The restrictions on the players were undoubtedly over-cautious. Perhaps it was right that they should be: it certainly made the players miserable. In truth, most players tend to have little enough curiosity about the places they visit: it is part of their dogged 'professional' attitude. But all they saw of Port of Spain was the cricket ground and the Hilton swimming pool.

In fact, the British High Commission arranged a trip for the players to go and see the scarlet ibis: a sensationally beautiful trip a short distance out of town. They laid on cases of beer for the boys, and invited all their secretaries so the lads would have friendly faces to talk to. But in the end, there were three guests on the trip: Edmonds, Frances and me. We enjoyed it immensely. Edmonds was quite determined to go, and was fascinated by what he saw: his attitude showed the major difference in attitude between Edmonds and the majority of the rest of the team: between the amateur revelling in every aspect of his trip, and the dour professional who hates it all and prefers to sulk round the swimming pool rather than run the remotest risk of 'ear-bashing' from outsiders.

The England players, have, in the main, lost the sense of the privilege of being cricketers travelling the world. There is little curiosity: if anything, there is often a subtle feeling of resentment of their hosts; a suspicion that people might want something from them lurks in every encounter. They don't want to be made a fuss of, they don't want to be polite. Much easier to stay in the Hilton.

Edmonds responds thus: 'You see, I have never seen cricket as a job. Touring has different connotations for me. But most of the guys are here to do a job of work, and in your job, you are always looking for the easy route, aren't you? Indeed, one had a sneaking suspicion that some of the besieged cricketers in the Port of Spain Hilton would have been simply delighted to fly home after the Second Test. Provided that they could have kept their money, of course.

Conspicuous among the disaffected England cricketers were some of the former members of the rebel tour to South Africa. When England arrived in Trinidad, and the team coach pulled out of Piarco airport to run the gauntlet of the protesters, the cry went up: 'Rebs by the windows!' The main argument of the demonstrators concerned them: the English rebels had been banned for three years. The West Indian rebels were banned for life. Does this, the protesters ask, represent the comparative value the two teams set on fighting apartheid? Meanwhile the West Indian newspapers carried arguments for and against the tour, bringing in all kinds of political considerations: and Edmonds, of course, followed all this avidly.

'I was amazed by one argument I met in favour of the tour,' he said. 'It was most forcefully put forward by a professor in a Jamaican paper, the *Daily Gleaner*. He said the tour should go ahead because it represented a chance to show black superiority – in short, the tour was a good thing because it gave a good opportunity for bashing whitey. He was going out of his way to promote a black-white conflict. That seemed terrible, to me. I found it very unpleasant.'

Gooch, as the rebels' captain, was naturally the main target of the demonstrators. The captaincy was rather thrust on him in South Africa, but it has made him the spokesman and apologist for the rebels. The imposed role has caused him considerable distress: he has become rather moody as a public person because of this. He is a sportsman out of his depth, for he is now a major figure in the international debate about sport and apartheid. His 'just professional sportsmen' line has not won him friends everywhere: his name is bandied about every time England prepare to play cricket against anyone other than Australia and New Zealand. It is nice, and convenient, to identify causes with names and faces, and it is Graham Gooch of Romford who is most closely associated with the problems of cricket and apartheid.

The problem will not go away, as Gooch is beginning to realise. During the trip to the West Indies, he grew particularly incensed by a statement from Lester Bird, Antigua's minister of foreign affairs, that referred to Gooch's own statement on apartheid. The statement, which did a lot to ensure Gooch's acceptability to the West Indies governments, was issued through the TCCB. Gooch was put out by the interpretation that Bird put on this statement. He wanted to speak out against this: in fact, what he wanted to do most was to tell the world that he had not made the statement at all: the TCCB had drafted the statement and he eventually agreed to it. He wanted very much to issue his own counter-statement, in mid-tour; one that would set his own views out with the utmost clarity.

The manager of the tour, Tony Brown, showed some perception in choosing to discuss this problem with Edmonds among others, since Edmonds has a better appreciation of political cause and effect than most. Edmonds' advice was uncompromising: 'Forbid him to say anything. If he makes any statement at all, the entire tour will be off.'

Brown managed to curb Gooch's urge to communicate with the world, and the tour rolled on. In the end, the story that reached the papers was that Gooch was utterly fed up with touring, and would not do so again. This was a piece of informed speculation: as I write, Gooch has made no official statement on this matter. It shows, however, that Gooch has grown weary of his international position. And it highlights the pressure the entire England side was under throughout the trip.

For they were denied the solace that most touring teams have available to them when political troubles strike: the compensations of playing cricket. The cricket at Sabina Park was a joyless affair, and that started the juggernaut of defeat rolling. 'We played the fastest bowlers in the world on a pitch that varied in pace and bounce – and that is a pretty lethal combination,' Edmonds said.

The hostility of politicians and bowlers was enough to make anyone yearningly homesick. People do not relish being called 'racists' – especially when they are not. 'But the people back home don't want to know about people feeling bad, do they?' asked Edmonds. 'And why should they? They have their own problems, they don't want to know about ours. So far as they are concerned, we are out in the sun playing a game and getting paid for it. And that is fair enough. But the team's problems are still there. Ideally, you *would* separate sport and politics, and you want to play the game in places where every one welcomes you. You want to play the best possible game and have the best team win. But when you arrive in a place to play cricket, and find there are 100 people at the airport shouting "go home", and every time you arrive at the cricket ground there are 100 more calling you racists, then it's going to affect you. You want to be received warmly. Even if 95 per cent of the people are pleased to see the team, the other 5 per cent make you think: "I'm not sure that I really need all this". And that attitude has crept through the squad. At the same time, I find the political demonstrations tremendously interesting. In a way, from the point of view of the interested onlooker, I'm almost disappointed that the thing seems to have fizzled out, and that we didn't get a bigger political reaction here.'

However, the demonstrators and the cricketers combined to give the England side a thorough mental battering. The match at Sabina Park even horrified those habituated to the ruthlessness of international cricket. John Woodcock (who is, perhaps, the finest cricket correspondent in the history of the game, and is unquestionably one of its clearest-eyed judges) wrote: 'The longer the match went on, the less like a civilised game of cricket it became. Except on that evening of ill fame at Old Trafford in 1976, when Close and John Edrich were subjected to such a disgraceful barrage by the West Indian fast bowlers, I think I have never felt it more likely that we should see some one killed.'

The ruthless intimidation of the batsmen, from openers through to tail-enders, is now a fact of life. Many cricketers, appalled, have suggested means of combating this. The painting of a white line halfway down the pitch, behind which the ball must not pitch, is a favourite suggestion. Another is the lengthening of the pitch to, say, 22 metres. Others favour more active intervention of the umpires, in support of the much-quoted Law 42.8: 'The bowling of fast, short-pitched balls is unfair if, in the opinion of the umpire, it constitutes an attempt to intimidate the striker.' Which could make at least half the deliveries bowled by the West Indian attack unfair. Botham and Thomas retaliated in kind, bowling bouncers similar at least in quantity. Surely, many writers say, something must be done to rule out intimidatory bowling.

'No!' said the bruised Edmonds. 'Load of nonsense. White lines down the pitch, lengthening the pitch, more intervention from the umpire – all nonsense. If the guys can bowl at the speed of light and send balls round your head, then they've got to do it. I'm not against intimidation. If you get six head balls in an over, that's showbiz. If you go out to bat, you've got to be able to take it.'

Nor does Edmonds bear any shadow of a grudge against Patterson for his brush with death – in fact, at a reception after the game, Frances met Patterson and said: 'Bad luck Patrick, better luck next time – and there'll be something in it for you if you succeed.'

There were veiled hints from some of the correspondents that Patterson's beamer was a deliberate ball that was prompted by Edmonds' slight altercation with Gordon Greenidge in the previous innings. Another Edmonds sledging incident? Well, no, another example of the Edmonds reputation running away with people, in fact. He and Greenidge were certainly embroiled, but not in a way either resented afterwards. 'I went in to field ultra-close to Greenidge, because he was getting on top of the bowling. Gordon has a substantial ego – like so many of us out there. He likes to be king of his own castle, and I think there was a sense in which he felt his virility was impugned by my standing so close. People have written that there was an exchange of words, and that he threatened to hit me with his bat. Not the case. He certainly got a bit stroppy, and he showed me the bat, demonstrating that he was still going to play attacking strokes, no matter how close I stood. People read more into it. It did upset him though: he played the next two balls in a markedly airy-fairy way and might well have got himself caught behind. I thought I was doing a good job there.

'As for Patrick Patterson, he is a young bowler, very excited at doing so well, and wanting to finish the innings off in the best possible way. He bowled five successive bouncers, all of which I ducked, and then, I think, he tried to send me the middle stump yorker. And his hand slipped. It was pure accident: but one that must have looked like pinpoint accuracy. I've seen Wayne Daniel

157

bowl the occasional beamer, quite unintentionally. I saw the West Indian team afterwards, and there were no hard feelings. I had a laugh with Gordon Greenidge about the incident.'

Edmonds' nerve was unaffected by this battering. In fact, he batted with commendable obduracy both before and after his encounter with Patterson, and at one stage was second in the tour batting averages, behind Mike Gatting who had to go home in mid tour for repairs after he had had his nose smashed by a Malcolm Marshall bouncer. Edmonds' attitude could have been profitably imitated by batsmen higher up the order.

'People have been saying, how do we score runs against these guys? So they have been going out and playing shots, and getting quick 20s. This is no good to anybody. What we should be doing is going out there to occupy the crease. We should be seeking to break up their momentum of taking wickets. They bowl expecting to take a wicket every four or five overs, instead of about every ten, which is more like the normal rate. Because of this, they are keyed up for every ball. We should be forcing the tempo to drop. Remember the fielding performances the Australians put up with Lillee and Thomson in their prime. They had a cordon of eight or nine slips, who were expecting just about every ball to come to them. They hardly dropped a thing all series, and took some fantastic catches. The momentum of getting people out every four or five overs was fully established: that's what we have to combat here.

'But instead, some of our batsmen seem to have the attitude that they're going to get the unplayable ball before long, so they've just got to get as many runs as possible before it comes along. It seems fool-hardy to me. Boycott, or Barrington, wouldn't bat like that.' The momentum theory works the opposite way, too. On the first day of the third Test in Barbados, the West Indies established the momentum of scoring runs and not conceding wickets. Because of this England – who, Lord knows, needed every chance they could – dropped three chances in the field, simply because they were not expecting wickets to fall. And Edmonds was, in fact, one of the guilty men that day.

England, however, did take one serious step forward into modernity on the tour, and one that Edmonds thoroughly approved of. They brought Fred. Fred was their bowling machine: 'A good player, though not very mobile in the field,' Gower said. Willis, assistant manager on the tour, was in charge of operating the device: 'I remember when you bowled like that,' I said to him. 'Yes, but my legs were stiffer.' Willis replied.

'Maybe Fred will help us to build a new race of super-batsmen,' Edmonds said. 'Batsmen who train by turning the bowling machine up to 100 mph and play it from 15 yards. I did a lot of work with Fred before I left, in the indoor nets at Lord's, all on the basis of ducking and weaving and occupying the crease. But the man who has impressed me most on this tour has been Allan Lamb. On the tour to India, his attitude was not the same, but here he is tremendously keyed up. The challenge of playing against the best and fastest in the world really means something to him: it really excites him. He practises with Fred with total dedication. It is really impressive to watch. Lamb looked on the verge of a big score every time he went out to bat, but somehow, it never materialised.

'But you cannot say that he did not give himself every possible chance to do well,' Edmonds said. 'And that may not be true of everyone.' Gower himself had his problems: he missed the first match of the tour and in the second he was out cheaply twice. 'So there were only two innings left before the first One-day International and so all at once he had a crisis of form on his hands,' Edmonds said. Indeed, Gower had a dreadful start. It says much for his uniquely Gower-esque qualities that he was able to re-find his touch and end up on top of the averages. But he could have done without the largely self-inflicted crisis at the start of it all. 'It was the same with Both,' Edmonds said. 'He has missed territorial games, and has therefore not been in the best possible nick for the internationals. Sure, Both has done his tremendous walk from John O'Groats to Land's End, but that doesn't get you fit for cricket. Cricket requires a very specific form of fitness. In an English summer, it seems that you are naturally fit, but the point is that you have played so much cricket for your county that you can't help but be fit. Out here, after months without any cricket at all, you need every game you can get to re-find your eye and your timing and your fitness. Had I been a supremo here, I would have selected my Test side, and sent them into the first territorial game of the tour. My priority would have been to play them all into fitness. Sorry, the rest of you guys: this is the Test team, winning Tests is my priority, and I want these guys fully prepared.'

Again, Edmonds makes the most obvious kind of sense. It seems –

especially in retrospect – quite incredible that England did not place a higher priority in giving the senior men as much practice time in the middle as humanly possible. Indeed, Geoff Boycott, out in the Caribbean as a journalist, showed more dedication to cricket practice on the trip than did some of England's players. When Boycott travelled as a player and filled in the 'purpose of visit' space on his immigration forms, he, alone of the England squad, would write 'business'. 'I can't understand these people sunbathing round the pool,' he would say. 'I like sunbathing all right, but I'm not here for pleasure. I'm here for business. And my business is making runs.'

Boycott was a somewhat incongruous member of the press box crew, but journalism seemed to be suiting him: he was in the best of spirits. We spoke about Edmonds, and he said: 'I've always been a great supporter of his. He should have played a lot more Test cricket than he has.'

There are always hosts of former internationals around Test matches, all bemoaning the state of the modern game. Edmonds, however, continued to bemoan the fact that the modern game isn't actually modern enough. The modern game is unquestionably bafflingly fast, potentially lethal, and genuinely profitable. Edmonds would like to see a greater appreciation of all these factors in the way the game is run. He is a great believer in technology. 'We can put a man on the moon,' he said, 'but we can still have terrible disputes about whether or not a ball touched a bat, or whether a ball would have hit the wicket. Sir Bernard Lovell has said there is the technology available to develop devices that will put an end to all such disputes. If that means that we will need an umpire in a glass box on the boundary, so what? Accurate decisions, and the ending of arguments, are what matter.

'And while I have nothing at all against bouncers, I am against the cynical slowing down of over-rates that has become part of modern cricket. The reason for this – so you can always have a couple of fast bowlers fresh – is unacceptable, and it is poor stuff for the crowds who pay the money. I would like to see a Law whereby teams were required to bowl at the rate of, say, one over every four minutes. Not a minimum number of overs in a day: this is open to abuse by the side bowling first. At the end of an innings, let us say the West Indies have bowled us out in 45 overs, but in that time they should, by law, have bowled 55. They should then be fined 10 runs for every over by which they fell short.'

I countered by arguing that this would mean a fundamental change of cricket thinking: you are not awarded runs, you earn them. The response to that was 'what about wides and no balls, then?' Or the five runs you are awarded when the ball strikes an abandoned helmet for that matter? Edmonds' notion is a harnessing of the same principle, and it makes sense.

But Edmonds cheerfully steps into outright heresy with his advocation of the limited over Test match. 'I want to counteract boringly inevitable fourth and fifth days,' he said. 'People want to see a result.' Edmonds, as ever, is full of startling notions: it is a healthier reaction to consider these on their merits than to suffer a kneejerk reaction of distaste. 'I know many people will find the idea of a limited overs Test match unacceptable, but in many ways it would be a good move. The format can be worked out. If you bowl sides out for less than their quota of overs, you could be awarded the residue of overs, and bat through them yourselves if you can.'

However, as we spoke in Trinidad, it was not the game of cricket that was in most urgent need of gingering up. It was the England team. Edmonds said: 'I'm conscious that for a few current players, being selected seems to be an end in itself. I have always said that with county players, there is a tendency to roll along from one game to the next: if you miss out on Tuesday then there's every chance it will all come good on Thursday. There is no sense of occasion about a county match. And in just the same way that by the time you are 35, your birthday is no longer the most amazing occasion in the world, a Test match ceases to be special for a regular England player. If you don't succeed in Port of Spain, maybe it'll be OK in Barbados. There'll be another Test match along soon enough.' In 1986 there were 16 Tests scheduled, and eight one day internationals. 'There is some tendency for players to drift from one Test to the next,' Edmonds said. 'Perhaps it would help if there were tangible rewards for victory: if the financial structure were a little different. If, say, there was a pool of £100,000 for the winners of every Test!'

If the last great amateur could bring that about, he would certainly win the life-long affection of his England colleagues. As I left Trinidad, however, the England team were not feeling noticeably affectionate towards Edmonds. In fact, he was at the the centre of a first class row. And it was all my fault. After spending months talking with Edmonds, and naturally discussing the various Edmonds rows, I can claim without suggestion of false modesty, that I caused an Edmonds row – all by myself and without any help at all from Philippe Henri. It demonstrated the persistence of the belief that Edmonds will always put himself in the wrong, and also the terrible, suspicious mentality of a cricket team undergoing a hammering.

It really was all my fault, though I certainly had a lot of help from the *Trinidad Guardian*. As England slithered and slid to defeat in the second Test match, the *Trinidad Guardian* ran a story reporting the criticism Botham had been receiving from English journalists. Most of the journalists had filed fairly unflattering pieces about Botham: he had a disastrous match, and bowled a quite dreadful new ball spell. The Trinidad paper ran a piece credited to both Reuter and the Caribbean News Agency, which naturally decorated their report with the most quotable quotes. Now, I was in Trinidad working on the book with Edmonds, and also working for *The Times*. And one of my pieces, along with those of a couple of other writers, was quoted prominently in the story in the *Trinidad Guardian*.

The England team, who don't get to see many English papers on tour, avidly read the piece in the *Guardian* – and some of them instantly leapt to the conclusion that I had been fed the piece by Edmonds. At a rancourous team meeting, Edmonds was roundly accused of disloyalty.

It is hard to say which of us was more insulted: Edmonds by these accusations of treachery, or me, by the belief that I needed a ghost writer to formulate my views. I had written my Botham piece before Edmonds and I had our long discussion on team meetings and the failings of the tour. But no: Edmonds was deemed guilty by association. This angry team meeting was followed by a yet more angry meeting between the press and the tour management. It was all caused by a few out-of-context quotes in the local paper. And it seemed to me that what England players had taken to heart was not the defeat, but the criticism.

Edmonds said: 'If a businessman had wanted to know what was being said in the English papers as badly as we seemed to, he would have found out for himself. We don't need to rely on reports in the local paper. We can have every cricket report in every English national newspaper sent out to us every day by facsimile transmission. Then we would know exactly who says what about whom.' Instead, however, the journalists' distortions are themselves distorted by players' rumours. The perpetually sticky relationship between players and press was further soured by these few lines in the local paper, and the habitual dressing-room distrust of Edmonds was increased.

There is a terrible distrust of all media men by most cricketers: the seniors teach the new boys to be suspicious, and the more newsworthy the player, the more suspicious he becomes. Indeed, to express mistrust of the press is to assume the badge of a true star. Edmonds is, once again, an exception. Most cricketers, and most cricketers in a losing English tour party, cultivate a loathing of the media. They ignore the fact that they get plenty of money for writing ghosted columns in the press, and they overlook the fact that the reason sportsmen get plenty of money is because they excite public interest. Public interest is created and nurtured by the media. You cannot logically be a wealthy sporting superstar and resent the media. But logic isn't the strong suit of sporting superstars.

Edmonds, however, with his unending interest in communications, undestands all this. He has his 'ghosted' columns, but he writes them himself, with pen and paper. Edmonds could not bear to do it any other way.

Television is also a medium that fascinates him, of course, and he is a fine performer. He worked as a splendidly trenchant summariser for ITV when they covered the all rounders' competition. In interviews he shows a tremendous self-possession: I remember one occasion on Wogan when he was asked about his affinity for rows. He allowed the camera to move close in on his face and his unturfed forehead, before saying, with enviably good timing: 'Well – even when I had a forelock I never used to tug it.'

He has a number of reservations about the way cricket is presented on television in England. He finds the presentation rather dull, and compares it unfavourably with Channel 4's package of American Football. 'People know nothing about the game, but it has grabbed them. You have got to catch people's interest in any game, and you do that by packaging. The American presentation of the sport, with the huge number of cameras, and the relaxed by-play between the commentators, is superb. There is a myth that BBC cricket presenters believe in: that you musn't badger the spectator with too much dialogue. Well, it's true that we don't want Jim Laker describing every detail of a ball trickling down to fine leg, when you can see the ball trickling down to fine leg on the screen. But to have two knowledgeable and interesting guys discussing the game: that is something else. At its best, it is enlightening.

'The spectator is particularly interested in the psychological aspects of the game. Not so-and-so must be feeling good, and so-and-so must be feeling depressed: they want to know, for example, what I am thinking when I bowl to Viv Richards, or Allan Border; or what Both thinks about facing Malcolm Marshall. You can do a number of interviews before the match, and run them when the pattern of play makes them relevant. They do that sort of thing in a limited way in golf, when you learn how Nicklaus had been planning to play the 14th as he walks onto the tee. They also do that with racing: when you watch the horses go down to the start, you hear Steve Cauthen discussing his horse's chance and how he plans to ride.

'But the cricket package at the moment is rather sterile. Television is the most powerful medium ever – and in my opinion, cricket is being sold short.'

There was no television coverage at all of the Sabina Park horror-show, which was a great pity: it would have been fascinating to see for oneself the terrors the batsmen had been facing. Instead, we relied on words, as in the dark ages: terrifically interesting, informed comment, but which fulfills a different function to watching the horrors yourself. By the time the tour had reached Trinidad, the English channels were showing basic newsreel coverage of the games. It was still not exactly fulsome coverage of a fascinating, if sometimes depressing tour.

Indeed, the last night of the Trinidad leg had the air of a wake about it. The team had bitched at Edmonds, the management had bitched at the press, and the press had bitched back.

England had lost their seventh match in a row to the West Indies, and Edmonds had endured a game of terrible frustrations. He and Emburey had bowled beautifully in tandem: Emburey got five wickets, and Edmonds two, with two chances, including a stumping, being muffed. So it goes. He had batted with calmness and competence. He had revelled in his cricket, in the challenge of bowling at the top batsmen, and had a fine battle against Richards. Richards had been rocking back and cutting good length balls off his stumps, which might have been demoralising for some, but Edmonds got him caught at slip in the end. He had relished the impossible chance of trying to bowl England to an unbelievable victory. And had ended up a frustrated man. Indeed, the combination of enjoyment and frustration has been the keynote of his cricket career.

It was interesting to speculate on whether England would have done better had they appointed Edmonds as captain. There would have been no tendency to drift under Edmonds.

But any such regrets were unspoken, as Edmonds and I sat on his balcony, finishing off the Johnnie Walker and the Hine cognac. 'I am still really enjoying this tour,' he said. 'Batting against these guys, trying to bowl them out. It's not work, to me. And I know I'll be more philosophical than I have been in the past if I am dropped. I didn't play in the one day international, and it didn't worry me. I carried the drinks happily. If I am not picked, it will probably precipitate my retirement, but that's OK. Not every one can play. I'll play this summer . . . and reserve my options. I might still be tempted to stay on. It would be difficult to turn down an Ashes tour. If I have a great summer, I'll go. If not, I'll retire.

'Because it's time to do something serious.'

I helped myself to a smidgeon more Scotch. 'Will you enjoy business when you're not playing at it, though?'

Edmonds swirled his glass, clinking the ice cubes. 'That, of course, is the question. I'll have to become much more serious in my application to the property business. I'd have to set up a property company, and I expect I'd become rather conservative in my business methods. No dabbling in secondary and tertiary properties. I wouldn't be anything like as flippant in my dealings as I am now.

'It has been nice doing both: playing cricket and doing business side by side. I know one thing that has kept me in the game has been my wariness of settling down, and becoming serious, and having kids – that is something that frightens the life out of me. But it's time to get over that, now. Plenty of good things ahead, but I'll have to be serious. It'll soon be time to be a bon travailler – and to stop being un joker qui joue au cricket.'

It is not only Edmonds' bourgeois Belgian relatives that find him un joker when it comes to cricket. For years, cricket has thought the same. The upshot of this is that, despite his splendid efforts of recent seasons, Edmonds has never completely fulfilled himself as a cricketer. England is meant to be the natural home of the eccentric, but Edmonds' eccentric, maverick nature has not made him loved by England's cricket establishment. Perhaps the problem is that the nature of his eccentricity is so un-English. Or perhaps people find Edmonds' eccentricity out of place in a team game – even though as a team game, cricket itself is something of an oddity. Individualism has always been a great part of cricket, since individual confrontations are crucial to its patterns. There has been something about the nature of Edmonds' individuality that has, for so many people, struck the wrong note. He makes team-mates feel insecure; he makes captains feel insecure. Many people are not sure of the common ground between themselves and Edmonds.

Edmond's cricket career has been a pattern of frustration. Frustration itself becomes one of the most addictive of drugs – as, indeed, does success. Edmonds has had his share of both intoxication, though not as much of success as he would truly have wished. More than anything else, he is dissapointed that he never had more than the most fleeting chance to prove himself as a captain.

But it is the pleasure of simply playing cricket, of playing up and playing the game, that will be the hardest to give up: the joys of confounding opponents with the old stock ball (the one that pitches leg and hits off), the delights of plucking ridiculous catches off the face of the bat from a couple of feet away, and also the dressing room camaraderie, the unending banter, the great joys of being part of the athletes' conspiracy of excellence. True, Edmonds has his stand-offish side, but he knows he will miss the cheerful, unsubtle pleasures of playing in a team game.

But for all this, it is success, conspicuous success, that Edmonds craves for. From his school days on, he has seen himself as one of life's over-achievers. But in cricket, that statistic-obsessed most quantifiable of sports, the Test match figures tell the story: Edmonds has not achieved all he might have done. It is likely that full time business – business being also a readily quantifiable pursuit

– will provide a kind of compensation. Edmonds is a man to whom success comes naturally, yet consistent success somehow eluded him over 15 years of cricket – despite being recognised as one of the most astute, intelligent and clear sighted men in the game. Edmonds was intended by nature to be a kind of renaissance man, displaying skills of debate, negotiation, struggle and mastery in dozens of fields at once: in business, politics, writing, speaking and games-playing. But this is an era in which the man of parts is considered an unacceptable dilletante: the narrow minded specialist with limited views and limited aims is all the rage. Edmonds the cricketer, with talents fizzing off in all directions and a precariously low threshold of boredom, is no more the very model of a modern day professional than is C. B. Fry. Perhaps C. B. Fry would have had the sort of ups and downs as Edmonds had he been playing at the same time. I wonder, though, as professional attitudes to the modern game harden yet further, whether Edmonds will be the last of this line. I hope not. Cricket needs it eccentrics, needs such singular men as Edmonds if it is to remain sane. The game will be infinitely poorer if Edmonds is, indeed, the last great amateur.

STATISTICAL SUMMARY

Phil Edmonds in First Class Cricket, 1971–1985

Compiled by Simon Wilde

IN FIRST-CLASS CRICKET

Season	Matches	Innings	Not Outs	Runs	Highest Innings	100s	50s	Average	Catches	Overs	Maidens	Runs	Wickets	Average	Best Bowling	5wkts Inns	10wkts Match
1971	14	18	3	213	56*	—	1	14.20	9	479	153	1045	45	23.22	7-56	2	1
1972	13	19	3	203	42	—	—	12.69	16	526	177	1214	34	35.71	4-64	—	1
1973	18	29	1	476	76	—	2	17.00	12	735.5	248	1593	61	26.12	6-42	4	1
1974	22	31	7	453	57	—	1	18.88	24	815.5	266	1888	77	24.52	7-38	3	1
1975	19	28	4	426	78	—	2	17.75	17	814.5	238	1946	75	25.95	7-48	5	—
1975–76 (South Africa)	13	23	4	365	73	—	1	19.21	17	615.3	193	1484	57	26.04	5-50	2	—
1976	26	38	5	892	103*	1	4	27.03	33	888	286	2029	88	23.06	6-67	4	—
1977	26	38	7	558	49	—	—	18.00	30	885.3	292	1899	81	23.44	8-132	3	1
1977–78 (Pakistan)	5	3	0	11	6	—	—	3.67	7	†154	28	449	16	28.06	7-66	1	—
1977–78 (New Zealand)	7	8	0	93	50	—	1	11.63	16	†183	58	385	17	22.65	4-38	—	—
1978	18	21	6	359	46*	—	—	23.93	15	503	174	912	60	15.20	7-34	2	—
1978–79 (Australia)	7	9	2	115	38*	—	—	16.43	8	†149	34	397	11	36.09	5-52	1	—
1979	15	17	6	490	141*	1	1	44.55	10	564.4	181	1230	39	31.54	4-30	1	—
1980	16	13	2	208	52	—	1	18.91	6	473	143	1125	38	29.61	5-94	1	—
1981	23	31	6	391	93	—	1	15.64	24	899	280	1814	73	24.85	6-93	3	—
1982	21	22	4	505	92	—	4	28.06	7	789	242	1768	80	22.10	8-80	3	2
1983	19	20	4	208	65	—	1	13.00	15	820.3	230	1974	92	21.46	6-38	9	2
1984	25	33	4	600	142	1	2	20.69	20	823.3	233	2096	77	27.22	8-53	2	1
1984–85 (Sri Lanka)	1	1	0	2	2	—	—	2.00	1	39	13	102	3	34.00	2-9	—	—
1984–85 (India)	10	11	0	239	49	—	—	21.72	4	459.1	175	917	29	31.62	4-13	—	—
1985	23	23	6	221	29*	—	—	13.00	22	850.1	243	1942	76	25.55	6-87	2	—
TOTALS	341	436	74	7028	142	3	22	19.41	313	11,981.3 and †486	3767 and 120	28,209	1129	24.99	8-53	47	9

All matches overseas were played for England teams on tour with the exception of those in South Africa in 1975–76, nine of which were for Eastern Province and four for the International Wanderers.

*Signifies not out of unbroken partnership.

†Eight-ball overs were in use in Pakistan and New Zealand in 1977–78 and in Australia in 1978–79.

FOR CAMBRIDGE UNIVERSITY

Season	Matches	Innings	Not Outs	Runs	Highest Innings	100s	50s	Average	Catches	Overs	Maidens	Runs	Wickets	Average	Best Bowling	5wkts Inns	10wkts Match
1971	9	12	2	148	56*	—	1	14.80	7	326.4	104	727	31	23.45	7–56	2	1
1972	8	13	1	118	24	—	—	9.83	13	288.4	91	692	18	38.44	4–93	—	—
1973	10	18	0	300	76	—	2	16.67	4	445	149	885	29	30.52	4–68	—	—
TOTALS	27	43	3	566	76	—	3	14.15	24	1060.2	344	2304	78	29.54	7–56	2	1

FOR MIDDLESEX

Season	Matches	Innings	Not Outs	Runs	Highest Innings	100s	50s	Average	Catches	Overs	Maidens	Runs	Wickets	Average	Best Bowling	5wkts Inns	10wkts Match
1971	5	6	1	65	38	—	—	13.00	2	152.2	49	318	14	22.71	3–42	—	—
1972	4	4	2	37	16*	—	—	18.50	3	184.2	70	402	14	28.71	4–64	—	—
1973	7	9	1	147	48	—	—	18.38	7	238.5	88	535	30	17.83	6–42	4	1
1974	20	27	4	393	57	—	1	17.09	19	752.5	248	1704	73	23.34	7–38	3	1
1975	16	23	3	394	78	—	2	19.70	16	676.2	204	1595	65	24.54	7–48	4	—
1976	23	33	4	711	93	—	4	24.52	31	808.3	264	1801	77	23.39	6–80	3	—
1977	25	36	7	518	49	—	—	17.86	30	868.3	289	1843	80	23.04	8–132	3	1
1978	11	14	2	233	43*	—	—	19.42	10	315	97	649	42	15.45	7–34	2	—
1979	10	12	5	398	141*	1	1	56.86	9	387.4	121	878	32	27.44	4–30	—	—
1980	15	11	1	177	52	—	1	17.70	6	449	140	1073	37	29.00	5–94	1	—
1981	23	31	6	391	93	—	1	15.64	24	899	280	1814	73	24.85	6–93	3	—
1982	17	18	4	406	92	—	3	29.00	6	675.4	206	1475	73	20.21	8–80	3	2
1983	17	16	3	145	65	—	1	11.15	15	733.2	200	1753	88	19.92	6–38	9	2
1984	25	33	4	600	142	1	2	20.69	20	823.3	233	2096	77	27.22	8–53	2	1
1985	16	16	5	155	29*	—	—	14.09	13	561	162	1252	53	23.62	6–87	2	—
TOTALS	234	289	52	4770	142	2	16	20.13	211	8525.5	2651	19,188	828	23.17	8–53	39	8

IN ENGLAND

	Matches	Innings	Not Outs	Runs	Highest Innings	100s	50s	Average	Catches	Overs	Maidens	Runs	Wickets	Average	Best Bowling	5wkts Inns	10wkts Match
	299	381	66	6203	142	3	20	19.69	260	10,867.5	3385	24,475	996	24.57	8–53	43	9

*Signifies not out of unbroken partnership.

171

STATISTICAL SUMMARY

IN TEST CRICKET

Season	Opponents	Venue	Batting 1st Inns	Batting 2nd Inns	Bowling 1st Inns	Bowling 2nd Inns
1975	AUSTRALIA	Headingley	13*	8	20-7-28-5	17-4-64-1
		Oval	4	7	38-7-118-0	6.1-2-14-0
1977–78	PAKISTAN	Hyderabad	4	—	24-2-75-3	30-6-95-0
		Karachi	6	—	33-7-66-7	
1977–78	NEW ZEALAND	Wellington	4	11	3-1-7-0	1-0-4-0
		Christchurch	50	—	34-11-38-4	6-2-22-2
		Auckland	8		10-2-23-0	45-15-107-3
1978	PAKISTAN	Edgbaston	4*		4-2-2-0	26-10-44-4
		Lord's	36*		8-6-6-4	12-4-21-0
		Headingley	1*		11-2-22-0	
1978	NEW ZEALAND	Oval	28	—	17-2-41-0	34.1-23-20-4
		Trent Bridge	6		15.4-5-21-2	35.1-15-44-4
		Lord's	5	—	12-3-19-0	—
1978–79	AUSTRALIA	Brisbane	1	—	1-1-0-0	12-1-27-0
1979	INDIA	Edgbaston	—		26-11-60-2	17-6-37-0
		Lord's	20		2-1-1-0	45-18-62-2
		Headingley	18		28-8-59-1	
		Oval	16	27*	5-1-17-0	38-11-87-1
1982	INDIA	Lord's	64	—	2-1-5-0	15-6-39-0
		Old Trafford	12		37-12-94-3	
		Oval	14	—	35.2-11-89-3	13-5-34-0
1983	NEW ZEALAND	Oval	12	43*	2-0-19-0	40.1-16-101-3
		Headingley	8	0	45-14-101-1	—
1984–85	INDIA	Bombay	48	8	33-6-82-1	8-3-21-1
		Delhi	26	—	44.2-16-83-2	44-24-60-4
		Calcutta	8		47-22-72-3	4-3-2-0
		Madras	36	—	6-1-33-0	41.5-13-119-2
		Kanpur	49	—	48-16-112-1	—
1985	AUSTRALIA	Lord's	21	1	25.4-5-85-2	16-5-35-1
		Trent Bridge	12	—	66-18-155-2	
		Old Trafford	1		15.1-4-40-4	54-12-122-1
		Edgbaston	—		20-4-47-1	15-9-13-2
		Oval	12		14-2-52-2	—

Having first appeared for England in 1975, Edmonds has played in 33 Tests out of the 105 his country has contested since then. His chief spells out of the England team have been: 1976 to 1977 (17 Tests); 1978–79 (5 Tests); 1979–80 to 1981–82 (27 Tests); 1982 to 1982–83 (8 Tests); and, 1983 to 1984 (14 Tests). He was also omitted from the first Test against Australia in 1985.
*Signifies not out of unbroken partnership.

SUMMARY

Season	Opponents	Matches	Innings	Not Outs	Runs	Highest Innings	50s	Average	Catches	Balls	Maidens	Runs	Wickets	Average	Best Bowling	5wkts Inns
1975	Australia	2	4	1	32	13*	—	10.67	0	487	20	224	6	37.33	5-28	1
1977–78	Pakistan	2	2	0	10	6	—	5.00	5	696	15	236	10	23.60	7-66	1
1977–78	New Zealand	3	4	0	73	50	1	18.25	9	792	31	201	9	22.33	4-38	—
1978	Pakistan	3	3	3	41	36*	—	—	1	366	24	95	8	11.88	4-6	—
1978	New Zealand	3	3	0	39	28	—	13.00	4	672	48	145	10	14.50	4-20	—
1978–79	Australia	1	1	0	1	1	—	1.00	1	104	2	27	0	—	—	—
1979	India	4	4	1	81	27*	—	27.00	1	966	56	323	6	53.83	2-60	—
1982	India	3	3	0	90	64	1	30.00	1	614	35	261	6	43.50	3-89	—
1983	New Zealand	2	4	1	63	43*	—	21.00	1	523	30	221	4	55.25	3-101	—
1984–85	India	5	6	0	175	49	—	29.17	0	1657	104	584	14	41.71	4-60	—
1985	Australia	5	5	0	47	21	—	9.40	8	1355	59	549	15	36.60	4-40	—
TOTALS		33	39	6	652	64	2	19.76	31	8232	424	2866	88	32.57	7-66	2

Opponents	Matches	Innings	Not Outs	Runs	Highest Innings	50s	Average	Catches	Balls	Maidens	Runs	Wickets	Average	Best Bowling	5wkts Inns
AUSTRALIA	8	10	1	80	21	—	8.89	9	1946	81	800	21	38.10	5-28	1
INDIA	12	13	1	346	64	1	28.83	2	3237	195	1168	26	44.92	4-60	—
NEW ZEALAND	8	11	1	175	50	1	17.50	14	1987	109	567	23	24.65	4-20	—
PAKISTAN	5	5	3	51	36*	—	25.50	6	1062	39	331	18	18.39	7-66	1
TOTALS	33	39	6	652	64	2	19.76	31	8232	424	2866	88	32.57	7-66	2

*Signifies not out of unbroken partnership.

STATISTICAL SUMMARY

WICKETS

Six wickets in an innings
8–53   Middlesex v Hampshire, Bournemouth, 1984
8–80   Middlesex v Sussex, Lord's, 1982
8–132   Middlesex v Gloucestershire, Lord's, 1977 (second innings)
7–34   Middlesex v Leicestershire, Lord's, 1978
7–38   Middlesex v Kent, Canterbury, 1974
7–48   Middlesex v Hampshire, Southampton, 1975
7–56   Cambridge University v Oxford University, Lord's, 1971
7–66   England v Pakistan, Karachi, 1977–78
6–18   Middlesex v Gloucestershire, Lord's, 1977 (first innings)
6–22   Middlesex v Surrey, Lord's, 1974
6–27   Middlesex v Lancashire, Blackpool, 1977
6–31   Middlesex v Nottinghamshire, Lord's, 1982
6–36   Middlesex v Nottinghamshire, Lord's, 1978
6–38   Middlesex v Derbyshire, Chesterfield, 1983
6–42   Middlesex v Warwickshire, Lord's, 1973
6–48   Middlesex v Hampshire, Uxbridge, 1982
6–49   Middlesex v Cambridge University, Fenner's, 1983
6–67   T. M. Pearce's XI v West Indians, Scarborough, 1976
6–70   Middlesex v Sussex, Hove, 1973
6–80   Middlesex v Kent, Dartford, 1976
6–87   Middlesex v Surrey, Oval, 1983
6–87   Middlesex v Derbyshire, Lord's, 1985
6–93   Middlesex v Derbyshire, Derby, 1981
6–93   Middlesex v New Zealanders, Lord's, 1983
6–111   Middlesex v Somerset, Bath, 1984

Ten wickets in a match
14–150 Middlesex v Gloucestershire, Lord's, 1977
12–120 Middlesex v Sussex, Lord's, 1982
12–120 Middlesex v Hampshire, Bournemouth, 1984
11–91   Middlesex v Kent, Canterbury, 1974
11–129 Middlesex v Sussex, Hove, 1973
10–72   Middlesex v Warwickshire, Birmingham, 1983
10–107 Middlesex v Hampshire, Uxbridge, 1982
10–129 Cambridge University v Oxford University, Lord's, 1971
10–161 Middlesex v Surrey, Oval, 1983

CENTURIES

142   Middlesex v Glamorgan, Swansea, 1984
141*   Middlesex v Glamorgan, Lord's, 1979
103*   T. M. Pearce's XI v West Indians, Scarborough, 1976

*Signifies not out of unbroken partnership.

174

STATISTICAL SUMMARY

Bowling in his first Test innings for England, against Australia at Headingley in 1975, Edmonds in his first 12 overs took five wickets for 17 runs. His victims were I. M. Chappell and R. Edwards (with successive balls), G. S. Chappell, K. D. Walters and M. H. M. Walker. His final analysis for the innings was 20-7-28-5.

Edmonds's best return in his Test career, 7 for 66 against Pakistan at Karachi in 1977–78, was at the time the best-ever for a Test innings in Pakistan and remains the best for England in that country.

Edmonds's analysis of 8-6-6-4 for England against Pakistan at Lord's in 1978 is one of the best in Test history: only Pervez Sajjad (4 for 5 in 1964–65) and K. Higgs (4 for 5 in 1965–66) had previously taken four wickets in an innings at less cost.

Edmonds was no-balled for England against New Zealand at the Oval in 1983 for bowling two bouncers in an over, a very rare, if not unique, instance by a slow bowler.

Edmonds performed the hat-trick for Middlesex against Leicestershire at Leicester in 1981.

In June 1983 Edmonds took 54 first-class wickets at an average of 12.33. He had not taken a first-class wicket previously that season.

Edmonds took his 1000th wicket in first-class cricket on 21 August 1984, for Middlesex against Leicestershire at Leicester, when he dismissed T. J. Boon.

Edmonds returned the analysis of 77-13-132-8 for Middlesex v Gloucestershire at Lords' in 1977 after Gloucestershire had followed on 263 runs behind. They had been dismissed for 80 in the first innings, when Edmonds returned figures of 16-6-18-6.

Edmonds has shared in three partnerships of 100 or more runs in Test cricket:

125	7th wkt	with D. W. Randall, v India, Lord's, 1982
110*	7th wkt	with A. J. Lamb, v New Zealand, Oval, 1983
100	7th wkt	with D. I. Gower, v India, Kanpur, 1984–85

Edmonds did not fail to score in any of his first 27 innings in Test cricket, his first 'duck' coming against New Zealand at Headingley in 1983.

*Signifies not out of unbroken partnership.

175

INDEX

PE refers to Phil Edmonds

Abbas, Zaheer, 134
Africa: PE's childhood in, 1–2, 4–9, 12–13, 18, 143
Agnew, Jonathan, 82
Allott, Paul, 33
Antigua, 148
Archers, The, 140, 141–2
Art of Captaincy, The (M. Brearley), 37, 66, 103
Ashford C. C. (Kent), 21
Austin Reed, 109
Australia: *v* England (1975) 42–4, (1978–9) 72–4, (1979–80) 80, (1981) 71–2, (1985) 44, 53, 54, 55, 90, 103, 123, 133–6

Barbados, 158
BBC World Service, 5, 82, 142–3
Bedi, Bishen, 49
Benaud, Richie, 59, 105
Biggar, Mike, 30
Bird, Lester, 155
Boon, Dave, 54
Border, Allan, 51, 57–8, 90, 123; duel with PE, 54, 55–6, 102–3, 110, 133–5
Botham, Ian, 33, 55, 75, 99–100, 108, 119, 150; and PE, 21–2, 123–4; against Australia, 44, 53, 54, 71, 133, 135; and Brearley, 63, 64, 71–2, 77, 103; Pakistan and New Zealand tour, 67, 83, 92, 93;

character, 85, 86, 122; commercial ventures, 112–13; against West Indies, 157, 159, 162
Boycott, Geoffrey, 74, 75, 77, 90, 113, 121, 158; and PE, 22, 66–8, 69, 160
Bradnock, James, 17, 18
Brearley, Mike, 22, 44, 50–1, 60, 61, 97, 151; England captain, 15, 37, 68, 72, 74–6, 103, 136; Middlesex captain, 28–9, 37, 39–42, 104; *Art of Captaincy, The*, 37, 66, 103; influences PE's career, 37, 53, 64, 77, 126; good relations with PE, 38–42; PE on captaincy of, 39, 70–1, 79–80, 126–7, 150; conflict with PE, 47–8, 58, 63–6, 68–70, 72–80, 103, 124, 132, 144
Brown, George (Ashford captain), 21
Brown, Tony, 87, 155
Butcher, Roland, 127, 148

Cambridge University: PE at, 23–4, 30–2; PE and cricket XI, 25–7, 33–4
Carr, Donald, 102
Chambers, George, 153
Chappell, Greg, 43, 45
Chappell, Ian, 43, 44, 45, 66
Congdon, Bev, 53
Cook, Geoff, 90
Cook, Nick, 98–9, 131
Coote, Cyril, 25
Cowdrey, Chris, 61

INDEX

Currie Cup, 44
Curtis, Alan, 102

Daily Express, xi, 33
Daniel, Wayne, 54, 57, 104–5, 126, 127, 158
Davies, Gerald, 30
Day, Sir Robin, 142
Denness, Mike, 123
Downton, Paul, 51–2, 62, 82, 132, 150

Eastern Province (South Africa), 44–5
Edmonds, Douglas (PE's father), 1–4, 5, 24; pro black African rule, 2, 6–11, 12
Edmonds, Frances (PE's wife), xi, 21, 57, 60, 74, 92, 103, 143; article in *Daily Express*, xi, 33; on PE's cricket career, 24, 38, 43, 93, 112, 119; meets PE at Cambridge, 32–3; on PE's business ventures, 45, 109–110; married life, 73, 82, 87–8; on PE–Brearley conflict, 76; in West Indies, 153, 157
Edmonds, Jean-Daniel, 8
Edmonds, Marie-Elisabeth (PE's mother), 1, 2, 3, 11
Edmonds, Phil (Phillippe Henri)
birth and African childhood, 1–2, 4–6, 8–9, 12–13, 18, 143; inside view of African politics, 1–2, 4, 6, 7–11, 12–13, 23; and conspiracy theory, 10, 81–2, 95, 141, 143; religious cynicism, 11–12; moves to England, 12, 15; at school in England, 15–20, 21; at Cambridge, 23–5, 30–2, 34, 66; interested in business, 24, 28, 35, 78, 81, 86; meets Frances, 32–3; joins Edward Erdman, 38, 110; business activities, 45, 59, 94, 96, 107–12, 115–16, 117, 118–20; married life, 73, 82, 87–8; 'information junkie', 81–2, 92, 140–1, 142; interested in politics, 82, 83–4, 92, 117–18, 139–43, 154–6
character: 1, 13, 17, 20, 77, 121, 132; aloof, 18, 21, 85–6, 128, 137; disrespects rank, 3; 'information junkie', 81–2, 92, 140–1, 142; loves confrontation, 55, 59; makes enemies, 14, 21, 30, 45; mistrusted,
77, 95–6, 136; naïve, 47, 100, 106, 144; one-upmanship, 39; reckless, 96, 98, 100, 105, 106; restless, 81–2, 121–2; self-confident, 23, 26, 29, 34, 35, 41
cricket career: childhood cricket in Africa, 5, 19, 39, 56–7; ability to captain, 14–15, 18–21, 33–4; and Zambian Eagles, 16; at Cranbrook, 18–20, 25, 71; and Kent 2nd XI, 19; and Ashford, 21; at Cambridge University, 24–7, 33–4, 134; all-rounder, 25–6, 124; joins Middlesex, 28–9, 34–5, 38–42, 48; career influenced by Brearley, 37, 126, 144; good relations with Brearley, 38–41; England début, 42–4; plays in South Africa, 44–6; withdraws from Test team, 46–7; dropped by England, 47, 64, 70, 96, 98–9; conflict with Brearley, 47–8, 58, 63–6, 68–70, 72–80, 103, 124, 136, 144; spin bowling, 49–62; 'Chanel No 5', 53, 65, 69, 76; concentration problems, 54–5, 124, 125; duel with Border, 55–6, 57–8, 102–3, 110, 133–4; amateur spirit, 59–60, 146–7, 153; the yips, 61–2; tour of Pakistan and New Zealand, 66–7, 83–4, 92; works well with Boycott, 22, 66–8, 69; on Brearley as captain, 70–2, 79–80, 126–7; in Australia, 72–4, 92, 93; World Cup (1979), 74–6; Middlesex vice-captain, 76, 95, 103–5, 128; stays with Middlesex, 78, 113, 114; unpopular room-mate, 81–3, 93; enjoys touring, 83, 86–7, 91–2, 94, 118, 153–4; discusses rebel tour of South Africa, 89–90; mistrusted, 15, 95–6, 130–1, 136, 162–3; bouncers, 97–8, 99; sledging incident, 99–100, 101; conflict with authority, 101–2, 106; benefit year, 113–14; advocates patronage system, 114–15; close fielding, 122–124; batting, 124–5, 126; dropped by Middlesex, 127; thoughts of retirement, 129, 165–6; tour of India (1984–5), 50, 53, 61–2, 92, 126, 130–3, 137; World Championship of Cricket, 90–1; against Australia

178

INDEX

(1985), 44, 54, 123, 133–6; and Gower, 64, 66, 136–8; tour of West Indies, 145–50, 154, 155–9, 161–3, 164–5; injured by Patterson, 145–6, 157–8; criticises England's organisation, 147–52; suggests changes in Laws, 160–1; on the media and cricket, 163–4; career assessed, 128, 144, 166–7

Edmonds, Pierre (PE's brother), 18, 20, 21, 45; African childhood, 4–5, 8, 11; education, 12, 15–16, 17; in business with PE, 118–19

Edward Erdman (chartered surveyors), 38, 110

Edwards, Bill, 27

Edwards, Ross, 43

Ellison, Richard, 135

Emburey, John, 56, 59, 70, 71, 76, 105–106, 123, 124, 126; against Australia, 44, 54, 74, 133, 135; compared with PE as bowler, 50–1, 58–9; rebel tour of South Africa, 89–90, 105, 131; tour of West Indies, 146, 150, 164

Engel, Matthew, 33, 54, 134

England: *v* Australia (1975), 42–4, (1978–9) 72–4, (1979–80) 80, (1981) 71–2, (1985) 44, 53, 54, 55, 90, 103, 123, 133–6; *v* India (1976–1977) 47, (1981–2) 88–9, (1982) 99, (1984–5) 50, 61–2, 90, 92, 126, 130–3; *v* New Zealand (1977–8) 66–7, (1983) 97; *v* Pakistan, 66; *v* West Indies (1976) 46, 156, (1984) 129–30, (1986) 145–7, 149, 150, 152–3, 155–9, 164–5; World Championship of Cricket, 90–1; World Cup, 74–6

Ferris, George, 148

Fletcher, Keith, 88, 130

Foster, Neil, 86, 133

Fowler, Graeme, 82–3, 133

Fry, C. B., 167

Galladari family, 107–8

Garner, Joel, 75–6

Gatting, Mike, 3, 76, 85, 92, 122, 158; Middlesex captain, 104, 105–6, 127; tour of India, 133

Gavaskar, Sunil, 47, 130

Gearey, Sir Eric, 117

Gilbert, Rennie High School (Lusaka), 5–6, 8, 12, 19

Glamorgan, 26, 27

Gooch, Graham, 33, 75, 77, 90, 97, 149, 154–5

Gould, Ian, 69

Gower, David, 3, 54, 59, 85, 113, 149, 159; and PE, 51, 53, 64, 66, 99–100, 123, 130–1, 132, 136–8; England captain, 129–32, 135–6, 150

Greenidge, Gordon, 157, 158

Greig, Tony, 43, 44, 46, 101, 111

Hadlee, Richard, 97–8

Hadley, Robert, 27

Hogg, Rodney, 37

Hudson, Tim, 113, 119

Hughes, Simon, 71, 105

Illingworth, Ray, 56

India: *v* England (1976–7) 47, (1981–2) 88–9, 99, (1984–5) 50, 61–2, 90, 92, 126, 130–3; World Championship of Cricket, 91

International Wanderers, 45

Jamaica: Test match (1986), 146, 152, 155–6, 164

Jardine, Douglas, 15, 72

Johnnie Walker, 102, 109, 132

Jones, Alan, 28

Kapwepwe, Simon, 7, 9

Kaunda, Kenneth, 2, 7, 9–10

Kendall-Carpenter, John, 15, 16, 17, 18–20, 21

Kent, 27

Khan, Imran, 105

Khan, Majid, 25–6, 27, 33, 34

Knott, Alan, 72, 86

Laker, Jim, 56, 164

Lamb, Allan, 50, 86, 135, 159

Lamb, Tim, 34, 41, 96

Larkins, Wayne, 75

Leicestershire, 20, 26, 27

Lever, John, 64, 73, 77

Lewis, Tony, 58

Lillee, Dennis, 45, 63, 101, 158

Lloyd, Clive, 120

Lock, Tony, 49

Lusaka, 2, 3

INDEX

Mail on Sunday, The, 131
Mallett, Ashley, 45
Marks, Vic, 108, 117, 131–2
Marlar, Robin, 53
Marshall, Malcolm, 158
May, Peter, 99, 102
Middlesex: PE joins, 27–9; captained by Brearley, 28–9, 37, 39–42, 104; success of, 40, 42, 105, 126; PE vice-captain of, 76, 95, 105; sponsorship, 109
Miller, David, 37
Miller, Geoff, 74
Monteith, Dermott, 71, 104, 105
Murray, John, 40, 41

New Zealand: *v* England, (1977–8) 66–7, (1983) 97; World Cup, 74

Owen-Thomas, Dudley, 27

Packer, Kerry, 15, 72, 110–11, 112
Pakistan, 66, 74
Parfitt, Peter, 40, 42
Patterson, Patrick, 145–6, 149, 157–8
Phillips, Wayne, 54, 135
Pocock, Pat, 132–3
Pollock, Graeme, 44
Popplewell, Nigel, 24
Port of Spain (Trinidad): Test match (1986), 146, 149, 152–3

Radio Moscow, 82, 140, 142
Radley, Clive, 101, 105
Randall, Derek, 67, 75, 106
Redmond, Gerry, 30
Rhodesia, 2, 7, 12
Richards, Viv, 47, 75, 152, 165
Robinson, Tim, 81, 132, 133, 138
Rose, Brian, 67
Russell, Eric, 40, 68

Saatchi and Saatchi, 113
Sabina Park (Jamaica): Test match (1986), 146, 152, 155–6, 164
Schmidt, Etien, 45
Selvey, Mike, 71, 104, 105
Shepherd, John, 125
Simmons, Jack, 113
Sivaramakrishnan, L., 101
Skinner, James, 7
Skinner's School (Tunbridge Wells), 15–16

Slack, Wilf, 71
Smith, Mike, 42, 68
Snow, John, 101
South Africa: rebel tour of, 15, 89–90, 97, 99; PE plays in, 44–5
South African Breweries XI, 15, 89–90, 97, 99, 154
Spencer, John, 27
Star, The, 131
Steele, Keith, 27
Sturt, Mike, 105
Sunday Times, The, 79
Swarbrook, Fred, 61

Taylor, Bob, 72, 88, 98, 99, 135, 137–8
Taylor, Chilton, 27
TCCB, 115, 155
Thomas, Bernard, 87
Thomas, Greg, 149, 157
Titmus, Fred, 40, 43–4, 56, 125
Trinidad: Test match (1986), 146, 149, 152–3
Trinidad Guardian, 162
Trueman, Fred, 57, 113
Turner, Glenn, 101

Underwood, Derek, 43, 51, 52, 57, 72, 124; rebel tour of South Africa, 15, 99; tour of India, 47

Vengsarkar, Dilip, 99–100, 101
Vonnegut, Kurt, 36

Walker, Max, 43, 45
Walters, Doug, 43, 44
Wessels, Kepler, 54
West Indies: *v* England, (1976) 46, (1984) 129–30, (1986) 145–7, 149, 150, 152–3, 155–9, 164–5; World Cup (1979), 75–6
Willis, Bob, 54, 64, 67, 68, 71, 74, 77, 131, 151, 159; and PE, 50, 59, 97–8, 99, 100; England captain, 88, 97–8
Wisden Cricketers' Almanack, 72
Woodcock, John, 126, 156
World Championship of Cricket, 90–1
World Cup (1979), 74–6

Zambia, 2, 8, 9, 12
Zambian Eagles, 16
Zia, General, 83–4, 92